Rob Willson is a cognitive behavior therapist in private practice. He is a tutor at Goldsmiths College, University of London, and studying for a PhD at the Institute of Psychiatry, King's College London. He holds an Honours degree in Psychology, an MSc in Rational Emotive Behavior Therapy, and a Postgraduate Diploma in Social and Behavioral Health Studies. He has been involved in treating individuals with health anxiety for the past thirteen years. David Veale and Rob Willson are authors of *Overcoming Obsessive Compulsive Disorder, Overcoming Body Image Problems (including Body Dysmorphic Disorder)* and *Manage Your Mood,* also published by Robinson, and Rob is author of *Cognitive Behavioural Therapy for Dummies* published by Wiley.

Dr David Veale is a consultant psychiatrist in cognitive behavior therapy at the South London and Maudsley Trust and the Priory Hospital North London. He is an Honorary Senior Lecturer at the Institute of Psychiatry, King's College, London. He is an accredited cognitive behavior therapist and was President of the British Association of Behavioural and Cognitive Psychotherapies from 2006 to 2008. He sat on the National Institute for Health and Clinical Excellence (NICE) working group that provided guidelines for treating obsessive compulsive disorder (OCD) and body dysmorphic disorder (BDD) in the UK. He has about seventy publications to his name, and his own website, www.veale.co.uk.

The aim of the **Overcoming** series is to enable people with a range of common problems and disorders to take control of their own recovery program. Each title, with its specially tailored program, is devised by a practising clinician using the latest techniques of cognitive behavioral therapy – techniques which have been shown to be highly effective in helping people overcome their problems by changing the way they think about themselves and their difficulties. The series was initiated in 1993 by Peter Cooper, Professor of Psychology at Reading University in the UK whose book on overcoming bulimia nervosa and binge-eating continues to help many people in the UK, the USA, Australasia and Europe.

Titles in the series include:

OVERCOMING ANGER AND IRRITABILITY
OVERCOMING ANOREXIA NERVOSA
OVERCOMING ANXIETY
OVERCOMING BODY IMAGE PROBLEMS
OVERCOMING BULIMIA NERVOSA AND BINGE-EATING
OVERCOMING CHILDHOOD TRAUMA
OVERCOMING CHRONIC FATIGUE
OVERCOMING CHRONIC PAIN
OVERCOMING COMPULSIVE GAMBLING
OVERCOMING DEPERSONALIZATION AND FEELINGS OF UNREALITY
OVERCOMING DEPRESSION
OVERCOMING GRIEF
OVERCOMING HEALTH ANXIETY
OVERCOMING INSOMNIA AND SLEEP PROBLEMS
OVERCOMING LOW SELF-ESTEEM
OVERCOMING MOOD SWINGS
OVERCOMING OBSESSIVE COMPULSIVE DISORDER
OVERCOMING PANIC
OVERCOMING PARANOID AND SUSPICIOUS THOUGHTS
OVERCOMING RELATIONSHIP PROBLEMS
OVERCOMING SEXUAL PROBLEMS
OVERCOMING SOCIAL ANXIETY AND SHYNESS
OVERCOMING STRESS
OVERCOMING TRAUMATIC STRESS
OVERCOMING WEIGHT PROBLEMS
OVERCOMING WORRY
OVERCOMING YOUR CHILD'S FEARS AND WORRIES
OVERCOMING YOUR CHILD'S SHYNESS AND SOCIAL ANXIETY
OVERCOMING YOUR SMOKING HABIT

OVERCOMING HEALTH ANXIETY

A self-help guide using Cognitive Behavioral Techniques

ROB WILLSON AND
DAVID VEALE

ROBINSON
London

ROBINSON

First published in Great Britain in 2009 by Robinson

7 9 10 8

A CIP catalogue record for this book is available from the British Library.

ISBN: 978-1-84529-824-1

Printed and bound in Great Britain by CPI Group (UK) Ltd, Croydon, CR0 4YY

Papers used by Robinson are from well-managed forests and other responsible sources

Robinson
An imprint of
Little, Brown Book Group
Carmelite House
50 Victoria Embankment
London EC4Y 0DZ

An Hachette UK Company
www.hachette.co.uk

www.littlebrown.co.uk

Important Note
This book is not intended as a substitute for medical advice or treatment. Any person with a condition requiring medical attention should consult a qualified medical practitioner or suitable therapist.

Table of contents

Acknowledgements

We would like to acknowledge all of the individuals who have health anxiety with whom we have worked. You have taught us much about this challenging problem, and are the inspiration for writing this book.

We would like to acknowledge all of the clinicians and researchers who have contributed to the psychological understanding of health anxiety. A far from exhaustive list of these includes Paul Salkouskis, Adrian Wells, Ann Hackmann, Steven Taylor, Gordon Asmundonson and David M. Clark.

Introduction

Why a cognitive behavioral approach?

The approach this book takes in attempting to help you overcome your problems with health anxiety is a 'cognitive-behavioral' one. A brief account of the history of this form of intervention might be useful and encouraging. In the 1950s and 1960s a set of therapeutic techniques was developed, collectively termed 'behavior therapy'. These techniques shared two basic features. First, they aimed to remove symptoms (such as anxiety) by dealing with those symptoms themselves, rather than their deep-seated underlying historical causes (traditionally the focus of psychoanalysis, the approach developed by Sigmund Freud and his associates). Second, they were scientifically based, in the sense that they used techniques derived from what laboratory psychologists were finding out about the mechanisms of learning, and they put these techniques to scientific test. The area where behavior therapy initially proved to be of most value was in the treatment of anxiety disorders, especially specific phobias (such as extreme fear of animals or heights) and agoraphobia, both notoriously difficult to treat using conventional psychotherapies.

After an initial flush of enthusiasm, discontent with behavior therapy grew. There were a number of reasons for this, an important one of which was the fact that behavior therapy did not deal with the internal thoughts which were so obviously central to the distress that many patients were experiencing. In particular, behavior therapy proved inadequate when it came to the treatment of depression. In the late 1960s and early 1970s a treatment for depression was developed called 'cognitive therapy'. The pioneer in this enterprise was an American psychiatrist, Professor Aaron T. Beck. He developed a theory of depression which emphasized the importance of people's depressed styles of thinking, and, on the basis of this theory, he specified a new form of therapy. It would not be an exaggeration to say that Beck's work has changed the nature of psychotherapy, not just for depression but for a range of psychological problems.

The techniques introduced by Beck have been merged with the techniques developed earlier by the behavior therapists to produce a therapeutic approach which has come to be known as 'cognitive behavioral therapy' (or CBT). This therapy has been subjected to the strictest scientific testing and has been found to be highly successful for a significant proportion of cases of depression. It has now become clear that specific patterns of disturbed thinking are associated with a wide range of psychological problems, not just depression, and that the treatments which deal with these are highly effective. So, effective cognitive behavioral treatments have been developed for a range of anxiety disorders, such as panic disorder, generalized anxiety disorder, specific phobias, social phobia, obsessive compulsive disorders, as well as for other conditions such as drug addictions, and eating disorders like bulimia nervosa. Indeed, cognitive behavioral techniques have been found to have an application beyond the narrow categories of psychological disorders. They have been applied effectively, for example, to helping people with weight problems, couples with marital difficulties, as well as those who wish to give up smoking or deal with drinking problems. They have also been effectively applied to dealing with low self-esteem. In relation to the current self-help manual, over several years effective CBT techniques have been developed for helping people overcome their problems with anxieties concerning their health.

The starting point for CBT is the realization that the way we think, feel and behave are all intimately linked, and by changing the way we think about ourselves, our experiences, and the world around us in effect changes the way we feel and what we are able to do. So, for example, by helping a depressed person identify and challenge their automatic depressive thoughts, a route out of the cycle of depressive thoughts and feelings can be found. Similarly, habitual behavioral responses are driven by a complex set of thoughts and feelings, and CBT, as you will discover from this book, by providing a means for the behavior, thoughts and feelings to be brought under control, enables these responses to be undermined and a different kind of life to be possible.

Although effective CBT treatments have been developed for a wide range of disorders and problems, these treatments are not currently widely available; and, when people try on their own to help themselves, they often, inadvertently, do things which make matters worse. In recent years, experts in a wider range of areas have taken the principles and techniques of specific cognitive behavioral therapies for particular problems and presented them in manuals (the Overcoming series) which people can read and apply themselves. These manuals specify a systematic program of treatment which the person works through to overcome their difficulties. In this way, cognitive behavioral therapeutic techniques of proven value are being made available on the widest possible basis.

The use of self-help manuals is never going to replace the need for therapists, and many people with emotional and behavioral problems will need the help of a qualified professional. It is also the case that, despite the widespread success of cognitive behavioral therapy, some people will not respond to it and will need one of the other treatments available. Nevertheless, although research on the use of these self-help manuals is at an early stage, the work done to date indicates that for a large number of people, such a manual is sufficient for them to overcome their problems without professional help. Sadly, many people suffer on their own for years. Sometimes they feel reluctant to seek help without first making a serious effort to manage on their own. Often they feel too awkward or even ashamed to ask for help. It may be that appropriate help is not forthcoming, despite their best efforts to find it. For many of these people, the cognitive behavioral self-help manual will provide a lifeline to a better future.

Professor Peter J. Cooper
The University of Reading, 2009

1

What is health anxiety?

Paul's fear of cancer

Following the death of his father two years earlier, Paul, aged fifty-six, became preoccupied with the idea that he would develop bowel cancer. He had known one of his father's friends to have Multiple Sclerosis and had become particularly afraid of the way it seemed to come and go without warning, leaving more permanent damage behind each time. Paul spent at least five hours a day preoccupied with his health. He had become acutely tuned in to his body for any possible signs of disease. He was especially anxious about any feelings of discomfort in his stomach, but he would often worry about other physical sensations too, fearing they could be 'secondary' tumors. At times he would be afraid that he might develop cancer, and in his more acutely anxious moments he'd become convinced he had the disease. Paul would check his stools when he went to the toilet for any sign of blood or mucus, and would frequently feel unsure that what he was looking at was normal. He bought several 'home detection kits' for self-testing for bowel cancer, and would sometimes feel reassured for a short while, but often wondered how reliable the tests really were. He would spend hours each day on the Internet looking for symptoms of bowel cancer, looking for reassurance that he did not have his most feared illness. He would also research health foods and ways of avoiding environmental toxins in the hope that he could reduce his risk of serious illness.

A doctor had told Paul that his symptoms were caused by anxiety, but he remained anxious because he couldn't find the 100 per cent certainty he craved that he was not ill or going to become ill. He would use books and the Internet to check lists of anxiety symptoms if he did ever feel any physical sensations he was unsure of. He would make frequent trips to see his doctor, taking with him notes he'd made of the time, bodily location, intensity and duration of his physical sensations. He never felt reassured for very long, and would often ask his doctor for more tests and screening, but also would worry that he could have a form of cancer that wasn't readily picked up on tests. Paul knew that he was 'a bit of a hypochondriac' and started to worry that he would have a 'cry wolf' problem, in that he'd had so many 'false alarms' that his doctor wouldn't take him seriously if he really were ill. He decided that he would have to give his doctor as much information as possible and to insist on another referral to a specialist to prevent this from happening. However, he could see his doctor becoming stressed when he saw him, and it occurred to him that perhaps his doctor knew he was ill and was too afraid to tell.

Paul's wife worked as a schoolteacher and had come

to dread checking her telephone messages at break times because there would inevitably be a message from Paul desperate to speak to her for reassurance. In the evenings Paul began to drink excessive amounts of alcohol to reduce his anxiety, but this put further strain on his marriage.

Paul suffers from health anxiety, and we shall return to his difficulties in other parts of this book to help illustrate the process of overcoming this highly distressing problem.

Defining health anxiety

Health anxiety is a condition that consists of either a preoccupation with having a serious illness or a fear of developing a serious illness, despite medical reassurance that this is not an issue. Only a health professional can diagnose whether or not you have health anxiety, but if you answer yes to the following questions, then you probably have health anxiety.

DO YOU HAVE HEALTH ANXIETY?

1 Have you been preoccupied with having or developing a serious illness for at least six months?
2 Have you had repeated reassurance from a doctor that you are not suffering from a serious disease?
3 Does your preoccupation with your health cause you great distress? Or does your preoccupation interfere in areas of life such as work or family and social life?
4 Do you repeatedly check your symptoms on the Internet or in books, examine yourself or ask others for reassurance?

Health anxiety is thought to be a spectrum, so even if you do not fulfil all the diagnostic criteria then you may be a person who still worries excessively about your health. The psychiatric term for health anxiety is hypochondriasis or hypochondriacal disorder, but we will not use that term in this book since it has a pejorative tone. It is derived from Greek and literally means the anatomical area 'below the cartilage'. This is because it was thought, at one time, that a problem in the guts of a person with hypochondria caused various mental disorders. In the nineteenth century, hypochondria acquired its more specific meaning of fear of disease and preoccupation with one's health. Sometimes the fear of becoming ill is driven by a fear of dying, which we discuss in more detail in Chapter 10. Another condition, which overlaps with health anxiety, is a specific phobia of vomiting, which we discuss in Chapter 11.

The onset of health anxiety can come at any age, though it commonly starts in adolescence or in young adults. Some people with health anxiety have an excessive worry about an illness, which is usually briefer in duration. However, the usual course of health anxiety is to come and go depending on various life stresses. Other people with health anxiety have a long-term or chronic health anxiety. It may be more common in women and occurs in about 5 per cent of patients attending a GP's surgery.

We shall discuss the experience of health anxiety problems in more detail below. Not everyone has the same experience of health anxiety – it partly depends on the severity of your problem and the culture you are from.

Physical sensations

The physical sensations that you experience are very real. Only you can tell people what you experience, so don't let anyone tell you the sensations you feel are imagined or all in your head. But some sensations (like dizziness or tiredness) often associated with a 'normal' condition may be misinterpreted as evidence of a severe illness. Thus a headache caused by tension may be interpreted as a brain tumour. A blemish on your skin may be misinterpreted as cancer. Feelings of unreality may be interpreted as a sign of schizophrenia.

Other people might have a long-term illness such as epilepsy or diabetes and have symptoms related to their illness but again misinterpret their significance. Such symptoms can be constant over time or change and vary in intensity.

Intrusive images

Intrusive images refer to pictures or a felt impression that just pop into your mind, especially when you are more anxious about your health. Images are not just pictures in your mind but can also be felt sensations.

Pictures are said to convey a thousand words and often reflect your mood. If you are very anxious, you might have mental pictures of going mad or dying. People often experience such images from an observer perspective, that is looking back at oneself and believing that the picture in one's mind is a predictor of the future. For example, a woman with health anxiety had an image of herself dead with her soul floating in space. This was frightening for her as she felt she would still having thoughts and feelings but would not be in control of the situation around her.

Images usually feel as if they are true or accurate and relevant now. This, however, is questionable, since such pictures may be linked to bad experiences and are like ghosts from the past, which have not been updated. So if you have had a bad experience of an illness in the family or of a doctor who had missed a diagnosis then that memory can become stuck in time and influence the present. To treat images as if they were reality can create many problems; to change that involves recognizing that you are experiencing only a picture in your mind, not current reality.

Intrusive thoughts

As well as intrusive images, you may have intrusive thoughts about yourself becoming seriously ill, dying or going mad. The threat to your health might be real or imagined and may be from the past (for example, a memory) or what you think could happen in the future. When anxiety dominates the picture, you may be overestimating the degree of danger to yourself or others. Your mind tends to think of all the possible bad things that could occur. This is called 'catastrophizing'. Your mind will want to know for certain or have a guarantee that you will not die or suffer from a severe illness. This leads to worrying about how to solve non-existent problems and to control as much of your bodily functions or to plan ahead to deal with all the possible problems that do not arise. The natural desire is to escape or avoid situations that are anxiety-provoking. One of problems is that your thoughts become fused with past experiences and accepted as facts in the 'here and now'. As a consequence, you develop a pattern of thinking that is like holding a prejudice against information that does not fit with your fears.

We'll be emphasizing the importance of recognizing that thoughts about your health are just that – thoughts, not reality. Learning to accept these negative thoughts and images willingly as 'just thoughts' and not buying into them is an important part of overcoming health anxiety.

Worry

Some people cope with health anxiety by trying to control their thoughts or suppressing them, which can mean the thoughts enter your mind more frequently. You may be worrying a great deal, trying to solve non-existent problems. These usually take the form of 'what if . . . ?' questions. Examples include 'What if I get cancer?' or 'What if I have heart disease?' 'How will my children cope when I have died?' Chapter 5 will help you 'think about thinking' in more detail and how you can best cope with your mind's invitation to try to solve such worries.

Brooding

You may be trying to 'put right' or make sense of past events by brooding on them, perhaps mulling over them constantly. You are probably trying to solve problems that cannot be solved or analyse a question that cannot be answered. When you become more depressed, you usually ask a lot of 'why?' questions. 'Why did I take those tablets?' or 'Why do I feel this way?'. Another favourite is the 'if only . . .' fantasies, as in 'If only I felt better . . .'. Alternatively, you may be constantly comparing yourself unfavourably with others and making judgements and criticizing yourself. Brooding invariably makes you feel worse because you never resolve the existing questions and may even generate new questions that cannot be answered.

Attentional processes

When you are worried about your health, you become more self-focused on your physical sensations and feelings and at the same time discarding negative test results. This tends to make you more aware of how you feel and makes you more likely to assume that your thoughts or pictures in your mind (such as an image of yourself being ill) are realities. This, in turn, interferes with your ability to make simple decisions, pay attention to or concentrate on your normal tasks or what people around you are saying. You are likely to be less creative and less able to listen effectively. When severe, it may make you feel more paranoid. Your view of the world now depends on your thoughts and the way these chatter away inside your mind rather than your experience. In other situations you may be so focused on monitoring your physical sensations that you fail to take in the context and find it difficult to concentrate on what others are saying. Chapter 6 will discuss ways of shifting your attention broadly and more externally towards reality.

Effect on feelings

Experiencing health anxiety is often a mixture of different emotions. Typically, the experience is of *anxiety* and varying degrees of *depression*. The problem is not that you are just anxious, but that your anxiety is either particularly severe or persistent.

Anxiety can produce a variety of physical sensations too, including feeling hot and sweaty, having a racing heart, feeling faint, wobbly or shaky, experiencing muscle tension (for example, headaches), having stomach upsets or diarrhoea, to list a few. These, too, may be further misinterpreted so that a vicious circle ensues.

If, however, you are becoming despondent and hopeless about the future, you may feel down or emotionally 'numb', feeling that life has lost its fun. These are core symptoms of depression. In addition you might start to experience sleep problems, lose your appetite and sexual interests. You might be brooding about the past, feel more irritable, and have difficulty concentrating. With depression, people can react by becoming withdrawn and inactive and wanting to avoid situations or activities that are painful. We shall discuss depression in more detail later.

Behaviors

People with health anxiety use a variety of different mechanisms to cope – which usually makes the situation worse in the long term.

When the fear is high, you may either try to distract yourself from your thoughts and feelings or to escape from or avoid situations that remind you of illness or death. Here health anxiety becomes like an illness phobia. For example, you might avoid going to the doctor because you are convinced you will be given bad news. You might avoid people who are ill, hospitals, doctor's surgeries, funerals, cemeteries, or reading anything about illness or death in the media. In this respect you may have so-called 'magical thinking', where you believe that simply thinking about bad events will make them happen.

When your doubt is high, you may make excessive 'checks' in the form of self-examination. Examples include checking whether:

- you have a lump
- your heart rate is too fast or blood pressure is too high
- you are losing excessive weight
- your nervous system is still normal
- you are losing your memory
- you can still swallow.

You might also be checking for information on the Internet or in books and in the media. Checking is an example of a 'safety behavior' that aims to prevent harm, increase certainty and reduce anxiety. People with health anxiety try to adopt ways to improve the way they feel but unfortunately the solutions usually leave them feeling worse and prevent them from testing out their fears. Safety behaviors are a way of 'trying too hard' to prevent bad consequences but often the solutions become the problem. We shall explore this further in Chapter 2 when we look at a psychological understanding of health anxiety. Needless to say, you have to stop all your safety behaviors if you are to overcome your health anxiety successfully.

You may be seeking repeated reassurance from friends or your doctor to find out the cause of your symptoms. When you are dissatisfied by one doctor, you may seek a second and third opinion and so on. Each doctor may order a new set of tests. Some of these tests may have ambiguous findings, leading to further tests. You in turn may become very dismissive or dissatisfied with your doctors. Interestingly, doctors can become frustrated with people with health anxiety and may prefer to refer you on to another doctor (rather than a mental health professional). Health anxiety has an effect on your friends and family, too, since when you are preoccupied with your health you may appear uninterested in anything else and distant. This in turn may lead people to become frustrated and fed up with you.

The content of worries, safety behaviors and avoidance behavior are closely related. When a person has to enter a situation that she or he normally avoids, then the safety behaviors start to reduce the potential for harm and discomfort. You may then try to avoid thinking about it by distracting yourself or suppressing the thought.

Extra problems with health anxiety

People with health anxiety often have other problems, which may make health anxiety harder to treat or to separate out.

Depression

The most common condition accompanying health anxiety is depression. Everybody feels down from time to time, but in normal circumstances the feeling usually passes fairly quickly and doesn't interfere too much with the way we live our lives. When most people say 'I'm depressed' they mean that they are feeling low or sad, or perhaps stressed, which are normal facets of human experience. However, when health professionals talk of depression, they are using the term in a different way. They are referring to a condition that is different from the normal ups and downs of everyday life. This is the type of depression we will be discussing: it is more painful than a normal low, lasts longer and interferes with life in all sorts of ways.

Depression nearly always occurs after the onset of health anxiety, suggesting that it is a result of the handicap and a frustration of one's fears. Often, individuals with health anxiety do not have full-blown clinical depression but experience a fluctuating mood, a sense of frustration and irritability. If you suffer from depression or fluctuating mood then you may also find it helpful to read our book *Manage your Mood*. After years of preoccupation and social isolation, individuals with health anxiety often have a low self-esteem which relates to areas other than their health. If this is a problem, then we would also recommend another book in this series, *Overcoming Low Self-Esteem* by Melanie Fennell.

HAVE I GOT DEPRESSION?

So how can you tell if you are experiencing depression or just going through a period of feeling low? Depression can only be diagnosed by a health professional, but to meet the criteria for a diagnosis you must have been feeling persistently down or lost your ability to enjoy your normal pleasures or interests for at least two weeks. In addition, you should have at least two to four of the following symptoms persistently. Tick off how many of the following symptoms of depression you've experienced in the past week.

CHECKLIST OF SYMPTOMS	
Significant weight loss (not because of dieting) or weight gain	
A decrease or increase in appetite	
Difficulty sleeping or sleeping excessively	
Feelings of agitation or irritability	
Tiredness or loss of energy	
Ideas of worthlessness or excessive or inappropriate guilt	
Reduced ability to concentrate or pay attention	
Reduced self-esteem and self-confidence	
A bleak and pessimistic view of the future	
Suicidal thoughts or attempts	

If you are suffering from depression, then your symptoms will be sufficiently distressing to handicap your day-to-day life. Your lowered mood will vary little from day to day, and will not usually change even if your circumstances do. However, it's not unusual for people who have depression to find that their mood is worse in the morning. Individuals' experience of depression varies enormously, especially among adolescents. In some cases, you may feel more anxious or agitated than depressed, or your depression may be masked by irritability, excessive use of alcohol, or a preoccupation with your health. Very rarely, people with health anxiety and severe depression may experience delusions of nihilism – for example they become convinced that their body is rotting, that they are already dead or that they have parasites living under their skin. More information on depression can be found in *Overcoming Depression* by Paul Gilbert.

Panic disorder

A person with panic disorder may also experience a number of worrying physical sensations such as palpitations, feeling short of breath or dizziness. The difference between health anxiety and panic disorder is that the symptoms of panic disorder can be easier to spot. Symptoms usually occur within 10 minutes and are often misinterpreted as evidence of an *immediate* catastrophe – for example death, suffocation, having a heart attack, or going mad now, rather than of a slow lingering illness such as cancer. When panic attacks persist they may lead you to avoid situations or activities where you believe you may have a panic attack, This is called agoraphobia. More information on panic disorder can be found in the book *Overcoming Panic and Agoraphobia* by Derek Silove and Vijaya Manicavasagar.

Medically unexplained symptoms

Medically unexplained symptoms (MUS), is a term used to describe a person who has multiple physical symptoms for which a doctor has found no physical cause. It is extremely common and overlaps with conditions such as chronic fatigue syndrome (sometimes called 'ME') and irritable bowel syndrome (IBS). The term 'medically unexplained' does not imply that there is no physical cause, but rather that there is no certainty about the cause – it may be physical, psychological or even social. Examples of MUS include:

- abdominal pain
- diarrhoea
- chest pain
- heart palpitations
- rapid breathing
- fatigue
- facial pain
- joint pain
- poor concentration
- muscle pain
- headache
- lump in throat
- wobbly legs
- ringing in ears.

MUS can overlap with health anxiety when the person becomes preoccupied with the idea that there *must* be a medical explanation for the sensation in their body or head and that it is a sign of serious illness or disease. However, many people are quite able to accept that their body can produce a sensation without ever having a clear medical explanation for it.

Obsessive compulsive disorder (OCD)

Obsessive compulsive disorder (OCD) is a condition that consists of recurrent intrusive thoughts, images or urges that the person finds distressing or handicapping. These typically include thoughts about contamination, harm (for example, that a gas explosion will occur), aggression or sexual thoughts, and a need for order. It is associated with avoidance of thoughts and situations that might trigger the obsession or compulsions. Compulsions are actions such as washing or checking, which have to be repeated over and over again until the person feels comfortable or certain that nothing bad will happen. Compulsions can also occur in one's head, such as repeating a phrase until you feel comfortable. There is often frequent avoidance behavior in OCD – for example, not wanting to touch anything that is contaminated.

Health anxiety is thought to be related to OCD. Sometimes the symptoms of OCD and health anxiety overlap, with a grey area between the two. Thus health anxiety may overlap with fears of contamination (e.g. from AIDS) but in health anxiety there is a greater preoccupation that one has or concern about contracting the disease. A separate diagnosis of OCD can be made if there are additional symptoms (e.g. if a person is continuously checking locks or needs order and symmetry). The recommended treatments that have been shown to be effective for OCD are cognitive behavior therapy (CBT) and certain types of antidepressants, which are discussed in Chapter 15. Therapy can improve the outcome for most people with OCD. For more details on OCD see our book in this series *Overcoming Obsessive*

Compulsive Disorder and in the UK the NICE guidelines on treating OCD.

Body dysmorphic disorder (BDD)

Body dysmorphic disorder (BDD) is a condition that consists of a preoccupation with aspects of one's appearance that is neither very noticeable nor seen as abnormal to others. Individuals with BDD usually feel they are ugly, that they are 'not right' and are very self-conscious. They usually have time-consuming rituals such as mirror checking. People with BDD are not vain or narcissistic; they believe themselves to be ugly or defective. They tend to be very secretive and reluctant to seek help because they are afraid that others will think them vain or narcissistic. Some people with BDD will acknowledge that they may be blowing things out of all proportion. At the other extreme, others are so firmly convinced about the nature of their abnormality that they are regarded as having a delusion. Since BDD overlaps with health anxiety, some people believe that not only is a certain feature ugly but that it is a sign of serious disease or allergy.

At least 1 per cent of the population may have BDD. It is recognized to be a hidden disorder since many people with the condition are too ashamed to reveal their main problem. Both sexes are equally affected by BDD. Typically, the most common concerns are with one's skin, followed by concerns about one's nose, hair, eyes, chin, lips or the overall body build. People with BDD may complain of a lack of symmetry, or feel that something is too big or too small, or that one feature is out of proportion to the rest of the body. Any part of the body may be involved in BDD, including the breasts or genitals.

Although women are more likely to have hair concerns (e.g. that their hair is not equal, that it's the wrong colour, lacks body or there is excessive body hair), men are significantly more concerned with hair thinning or baldness. The sex differences also occur with body size and shape. Women are more likely to be preoccupied by their breasts, hips, weight and legs, usually believing that they are too large or fat. In contrast, men are more likely to be preoccupied with their body build, which has also been described as muscle dysmorphia. Many individuals with BDD have repeatedly sought treatment from dermatologists or cosmetic surgeons, often with little satisfaction, before finally accepting psychological help. The recommended treatments that have been shown to be effective for BDD are cognitive behavior therapy (CBT) and certain types of antidepressants, which are discussed in Chapter 15. For more details on BDD see our book in this series, *Overcoming Body Image Problems including Body Dysmorphic Disorder* and in the UK the NICE guidelines on treating OCD and BDD.

Generalized anxiety disorder

Generalized anxiety disorder (GAD) is a condition characterized by persistent worry that is difficult to control. However, individuals with GAD often describe themselves as 'being a worrier' all their lives and seek help only when their condition has become severe and uncontrollable. For a diagnosis of GAD to be made, the anxiety should occur most of the time and be focused not only on health. For most people with GAD, the content of the worries are most commonly about relationships, health or money, but this often varies. People usually experience some of the following feelings most of the time:

- restlessness or feeling keyed up or on edge
- being easily fatigued
- difficulty concentrating or mind going blank
- irritability
- muscle tension (for example, headaches)
- sleep disturbance (difficulty falling or staying asleep, or restless, unsatisfying sleep).

GAD can also cause a number of physical symptoms and interfere with your ability to function normally. It is a very common problem either alone or in combination with depression on health anxiety. For more information see *Overcoming Worry* by Kevin Meares and Mark Freeston in this series.

Alcohol, substance misuse and faddy eating

Sometimes people 'cope' with health anxiety by consuming excessive alcohol or illegal drugs such as cannabis or stimulants like cocaine. However, the alcohol or drugs then become problems in themselves, since cannabis or stimulants increase paranoia and depressed mood and decrease motivation. To benefit from therapy, individuals will usually need to stop drinking or using substances first, because these will interfere with the therapy. Illegal substances such as cannabis may also be the trigger for the onset of health anxiety.

People with health anxiety (like the rest of us) will find it better to follow a healthy lifestyle. Interestingly, people with health anxiety do not generally follow a healthier lifestyle than the rest of the population – for example they are just as likely to smoke, drink too much coffee or alcohol, or be inactive. Sometimes health anxiety can lead to extremely unhealthy behavior either because:

- you are following a very restricted lifestyle or a rigid diet in the belief that it may cure your medical problem or an allergy, or
- you may be eating a junk diet or neglecting yourself as your mood becomes worse.

We are not saying that a poor diet is *the* cause of your health anxiety or depression, or that if you eat healthily you will not get anxious and depressed in the first place. There are of course many people in the world who follow a poor diet and are not anxious or depressed. Equally, some individuals with anxiety or depression have a healthy diet. But we do say that some people with anxiety or depression may be more sensitive to a poor and chaotic diet and that this is likely to be another factor in keeping them anxious and depressed. A poor diet can aggravate your feeling low, bloated and tired. Giving your brain and body regular and healthy food is an important step you can take to give yourself the best conditions for recovering from anxiety and mood swings.

It is important to avoid substances that will make your mood or anxiety worse or reduce the quality of sleep.

Olfactory reference syndrome

Olfactory reference syndrome (ORS) is a term used to describe an individual who is preoccupied by body odour, bad breath or the smell of flatulence which are *not* noticeable to others. This is sometimes regarded as part of health anxiety. Such individuals may use perfume to hide the presumed odour. They frequently shower, brush their teeth, change their clothes and ultimately avoid public and social situations where they think their body odour will be noticed. Some people seek frequent reassurance about their body odour. Others have marked avoidance of being around people and are housebound. Some people with health anxiety are also preoccupied with their body odour, which blends easily with their preoccupation with aspects of their health. For example, if you believe you have a terrible illness, it is not surprising if you also believe that you smell disgusting.

Famous figures with health anxiety

If you have health anxiety, then you are not alone. Some of the figures throughout history that have been reported as having health anxiety include:

- Florence Nightingale (feared illness)
- Charles Darwin (preoccupied with fatigue and gut problems)

- poet Alfred Lord Tennyson (preoccupied with fear that his eyesight might fail)
- philosopher Emmanuel Kant (preoccupied with his breathing and headaches)
- Adolf Hitler (became convinced that he had throat cancer despite doctors' reassurance)

Treatments for health anxiety

Until relatively recently, health anxiety was regarded as a chronic disorder that was distressing to both patient and doctor. It was regarded as being difficult to treat, because medicine had little to offer other than reassurance. This stance has now changed and the good news is that health anxiety is a highly treatable problem. This book outlines some of the principles of cognitive behavior therapy that are used in overcoming health anxiety, and we hope that it will help you aim to make a full recovery.

It's true that health anxiety can be tough to overcome and can call for a lot of hard work, but this is far from impossible for most people. As we'll show, a good amount of recovery in fact comes from working considerably less hard and from stopping your current solutions. What's more, getting on with other rewarding, productive and enjoyable aspects of your life is an integral part of recovery and will help drive health anxiety out of your life.

Cognitive behavior therapy (CBT)

CBT has its roots in 'Behavior Therapy', which was established in the 1950s. Later, Albert Ellis ('Rational Emotive Behavior Therapy') and Aaron T. Beck ('Cognitive Therapy') suggested that emotional problems were maintained by negative thinking *and* unhelpful patterns of behavior. CBT involves techniques of identifying negative thoughts and styles of thinking, and learning to question the content of such thoughts so that alternatives can be tested out. This method of treating depression was found to be as effective as antidepressant medication, and was then adapted to treat different problems such as panic attacks and obsessive compulsive disorder. Particular emphasis is laid on the 'homework' that you do to practise your skills between sessions. Because in this sense 'self-help' has always been at the heart of CBT, a number of self-help books have been produced.

CBT has been adapted for health anxiety and has been shown to be effective for adults in various scientific studies. This book is based upon the principles of CBT and is ideally used with the support of an appropriately trained health care professional (see Appendix 1). However, with the support of a friend, family member, or even alone change *is* possible. Many people with health anxiety find that they may have to wait many months to see a therapist, so getting started with self-help can be a really good first step. At present, there is no evidence that general counselling, psychodynamic therapy or hypnotherapy are effective for health anxiety. This does not mean that such therapies are ineffective but that they have not been investigated. It also means that people with health anxiety should first be offered CBT from a competent practitioner following a treatment manual for health anxiety, because this has been shown to be effective.

Effective CBT for health anxiety usually contains the following components, although it may not be necessary to use all of them:

- Understanding the link between physical sensations, thinking, attention, emotion, and behavioral components of your own health anxiety. This will be covered in more detail in Chapter 2.
- Testing out your fears and resisting doing the things you do try and feel more reassured (e.g. checking, researching information on the Internet , reassurance-seeking, seeking medical investigations). This will be covered in more detail in Chapter 7.
- Practising allowing catastrophic thoughts and images about illness or dying without responding or 'engaging' (trying to get rid of them, planning, examining, reassuring yourself, etc.).
- Learning to re-focus your attention away from your body and on to the environment around you. This will be covered in more detail in Chapter 6.
- Becoming aware of unhelpful thoughts and attitudes you have towards illness or death. This will be covered in more detail in Chapter 4.
- Learning to tolerate uncertainty and reduce excessive responsibility. This can help with reducing your

excessive fear of missing an important symptom. This will be covered in more detail in Chapter 4.

- Learning to spot yourself engaging in worrying about your health and to bring your mind back into dealing with real life in the here-and-now. This will be covered in more detail in Chapter 5.
- Putting time and energy back into things that are important to you. This will be covered in more detail in Chapter 3.
- Developing a sensible plan for taking appropriate care of your health. This will be covered in more detail in Chapter 13.
- Dealing effectively with the fact that you will one day die, without excessively worrying about it. This will be covered in more detail in Chapter 10.
- The type of health anxiety that focuses on a phobia of vomiting is covered in Chapter 11.

Medication for health anxiety

Antidepressant medication (a selective serotonergic reuptake inhibitor – 'SSRI') is not usually recommended for mild to moderate symptoms of health anxiety. However, if a patient's doctor believes that the health anxiety symptoms are likely to get worse (or if the symptoms have lasted for a long time) medication may still be recommended. Antidepressant medication is also sometimes recommended as an option in treating more severe symptoms of health anxiety, especially when depression is present. However, antidepressants can be helpful in moderate to severe health anxiety in the absence of depression. We discuss the use of medication in more detail in Chapter 15.

Combining medication with CBT

In general, we do not recommend using medication as the only remedy for health anxiety because there is usually a higher rate of relapse when a person stops taking the medication. Results tend to be better when the medication is combined with CBT (and for relapse prevention purposes most people need to take medication for at least a year, which may be beyond the course of therapy). This said, given that there are many different types of health anxiety, some people may do fine on medication alone and get back to a normal life with just that. Whatever approach you take, make sure you monitor your progress using the rating scales in this book so you can decide (with your therapist or doctor) what is helping and whether to try something else.

2

How health anxiety develops and is maintained

Although we are confident that health anxiety can be overcome, there is undoubtedly still more to learn about *why* some people experience it in the first place. Researchers and clinicians are interested in such research because it will help to prevent people from developing health anxieties. Nevertheless, if you already have this anxiety we hope that this chapter will help you develop a greater understanding of your problem and become more compassionate towards yourself.

Possible contributing factors

When considering possible causes for your symptoms of health anxiety, it is usually helpful to think of three groups of factors, those that:

1 have made you vulnerable to developing symptoms (for example, childhood experience of illness, trauma, genetic inheritance and unknown factors)

2 have triggered your symptoms (such as experiencing a health problem in yourself or someone close to you, or life stressors)
3 have helped maintain your symptoms (for example, the way you react, with particular patterns of thinking and acting).

What makes a person vulnerable to developing health anxiety?

As mentioned before, health anxiety might result from factors that make you vulnerable to anxiety and the presence of one or more triggers. Vulnerability to a health anxiety can be due to three types of factors:

1 physical conditions, including medical, biological and genetic causes
2 personality or psychological traits
3 life experiences.

There is a certain amount of overlap between these factors. For example, the way we respond to live events is influenced by our personality, which in turn affects the course of those events. The way we respond emotionally to events is influenced by what past events they remind us of. The way we are built physically may affect the way we respond to stress, which can then affect our emotional and behavioral reactions. The possible interactions are endless. When considering possible causes of health anxiety, it's important to remember that these factors all interact with each other. Imagine that the cause of a health anxiety is like a cocktail in a glass. The quantities of ingredients of the cocktail will be different for each individual and they will also mix and interact in different ways.

Genetic factors

A mental health problem can sometimes run in families. For instance, if you have a close relative who has had depression or obsessive compulsive disorder, you may be at slightly increased risk of experiencing a health anxiety at some time in your life. But you should bear in mind that mental disorder in the family is fairly common, and having a genetic factor does not inevitably mean that you will develop a health anxiety without additional factors. Similarly, it is possible to develop health anxiety without any evidence of genetic risk, so there is no point in worrying that you may be at greater risk than other people.

Chemical factors

Some doctors and researchers who work with health anxiety and depression focus on the role of chemicals in the brain such as serotonin. These chemicals are part of the nervous system and allow one nerve to communicate with another. Serotonin plays a part in many aspects of normal human functioning, including appetite, sexual desire and mood, so it is not unique to anxiety.

List here any emotional problems you think may come from your family history (e.g. 'my grandfather had depression', 'my brother had OCD'):

Medication that helps to enhance activity in nerves that use serotonin can ease symptoms of health anxiety, depression and OCD, and we shall look at such drugs in detail in Chapter 15. However, just because drugs that increase serotonin in the brain can help, it does not mean that a deficiency of serotonin necessarily causes health anxiety. This is like saying that if aspirin improves headaches, then headaches are caused by a deficiency of aspirin. The changes in serotonin levels are likely to occur as a consequence of your mind trying to dampen down your level of anxiety. If your anxiety level or mood improves, then it may help you to cope better and to face up to and deal constructively with any difficulties you may have.

Even if a doctor recommends that you take medication, there is nothing to stop you helping yourself by also using the approaches described in this book. These will involve developing a more compassionate and caring view of yourself, acting as if you truly believe you do not have to be excessively worried about your health, and doing more of the activities you are currently avoiding.

Brain activity factors

Health anxiety can be regarded an overloaded system, with your mind trying too hard to solve what it thinks is an actual or potential physical illness. In such cases, your mind's solutions become the problem. The system is overloaded because of the way you try to escape from unpleasant thoughts, images and feelings, or the way you try to control your feelings by worrying about all the bad things that could occur. This process can be seen in abnormal brain scans and serotonin activity. In our opinion, these biological changes do not cause health anxiety but are more of a reaction to it – the consequence of the mind desperately trying to escape from and control the way you feel.

This is not to say that the biology is not important – it does become part of the process of maintaining health anxiety. For example, when you are stressed, a stress hormone called cortisol goes up, and over time this will reduce your serotonin levels. As your serotonin goes down, you may feel more tired. This will affect your sleep and the next day this, in turn, will affect the way you cope with everyday events. Your body and your mind work together, one having an effect on the other. However, you can reduce these biological responses by acting *against* the way you feel (for example by not checking), and this will lead to better feelings.

Personality factors

Certain aspects of your personality may make you more vulnerable to developing health anxiety. For example, you may have always been a worrier and find it difficult to tolerate uncertainty. Such traits, in combination with one or more triggers, can make you more vulnerable to developing a health anxiety. There is, of course, some intermixing of the factors: it is clear that certain aspects of temperament are in part genetically determined.

Life experience

Much of our development occurs without our being aware of it, as we are exposed to literally millions of moments of learning. It is utterly impossible to unravel or organize them into a causal order. However, it's likely that some of

List here any of your personality traits that you think may make you vulnerable to health anxiety:

your experiences from a young age until now have helped train your brain in an unhelpful way, making you vulnerable to developing health anxiety. You may well have had experiences in life that have influenced:

- your beliefs and attitudes about health, death and disease (such as how careful you should be, tolerance of doubt)
- how much attention you pay to illness and to your body
- your sense of how robust or fragile your body is
- your responses to health concerns (e.g. how quickly you should see a doctor).

Here are some examples of the kinds of experiences that people we meet who have health anxiety describe as having contributed to their preoccupation:

- a family member being severely ill when you were growing up.
- being over-protected as a child, especially from illness.
- being over-protected as a child from deaths, funerals, illnesses in the family.
- being severely ill as a child.

You may have been brought up in a family with unspoken rules like 'You don't have anything if you don't have your health,' or 'You can't be too careful when it comes to your health'. You are likely to have learnt these rules, and they now influence your behavior.

What do you identify as your own life experiences that may have contributed to your being vulnerable to health anxiety?

What can trigger health anxiety?

Although it can occur at any age, health anxiety most commonly develops in early adulthood. The most common triggers for a health anxiety are:

- stress
- illness
- recovering from illness
- illness of a family member
- loss of a family member

- exposure to disease related information through the media
- exposure to disease related information through medical training.

Sometimes health anxiety seems to occur out of the blue, without any identifiable trigger or social factors, and may sometimes be triggered by a panic attack that raises a person's fear of and focus upon certain bodily or mental sensations. We've also noticed that some people have their first experience of health anxiety when things are going rather well for them, such as recently becoming happily married, enjoying their job, or having a really enjoyable holiday. In these instances people report having had a thought like 'wouldn't it be awful if something happened to me that spoils it all'.

What can you identify as one or more triggers for the beginning of your health anxiety?

HEALTH WARNING 1: UNDERSTANDING IS NOT ENOUGH!

Many people we meet in our social lives and at work still believe that the answer to an emotional problem is to 'understand where it comes from'. This idea is based on the assumption that there is clearly identifiable past event to which a person's problem can be traced, and that once the sufferer recalls this, the magic of 'insight' will lead to a short-lived outpouring of emotion and lasting recovery. How we wish it were that easy! This popular myth is decades old, and should urgently be updated. In 'Overcoming Health Anxiety – The Movie' it probably will happen this way, but in real life it takes much more work to rehabilitate your mind.

HEALTH WARNING 2: TRYING TOO HARD TO UNDERSTAND YOUR HEALTH ANXIETY CAN MAKE YOU WORSE

Spending too much time trying to work out the exact 'cause' of your own health anxiety may lead you to avoid other feelings and prevent you from trying to solve the real problem of not doing what you value in life. Some of the causes of health anxiety may simply be 'unknown' and buried in many years of life experience, personality factors, genetic factors or even factors as yet undiscovered by science. However, for most people the factors that have contributed to health anxiety are fairly straightforward. They can include your temperament, genetic predisposition, the way you react and how you cope – all of which will determine whether or not you develop a health anxiety.

A psychological understanding of the development of your health anxiety can therefore help you to take a more sympathetic, compassionate view of yourself, and thus make your attempts to recover more effective. However, exploring possible root causes ought to be a relatively brief process – when you fall down a hole, you don't need to know the exact route by which you arrived at the bottom in order to climb out again. The next step is to move on from 'why' you have health anxiety on to 'how' you are going to overcome it. And that, of course, this is what this book is really about.

What maintains health anxiety?

Theory A versus theory B

The essence of overcoming health anxiety using the various techniques outlined throughout this book is to gather evidence to find out whether the results of your experiment fit your existing explanation for your problems or whether an alternative fits better. In health anxiety there are two broad alternatives to be tested:

> **Theory A:** *I have a medical condition. My solution is to take every possible step to monitor my health, avoid anything that might remind me of death and to keep checking for information and seeking reassurance.*
>
> **Theory B:** *I have an emotional problem with being excessively worried by my health and my 'solutions' have become my problem and feed my worry.*

It may seem to you that Theory A works because you are doing something with the tools you have and you are stopping bad events from happening. The activities are learnt (like a habit) and can be difficult to break. It is therefore likely that you will avoid or escape from unpleasant thoughts and situations in the future because such behavior has been learnt; it has apparently been successful and given you a 'pay-off'. We are not saying that this is wrong or bad. It just happens because human beings, like other animals, can train themselves to think and behave in a particular way.

Try thinking of your own health anxiety problem in terms of two competing theories. Remember that only one theory can be correct – they can't both be true. In the space overleaf, write under 'Theory A' how you have viewed the problem, and how it has led to your using avoidance and safety behaviors. Then write against 'Theory B' another way of looking at your experience that would enable you to test your alternative.

If you have a health anxiety problem, you will probably have been following Theory A for some time. However, in order to determine whether Theory B might be a more helpful explanation for your problems, you will have to act *as if* it were correct (even if you don't believe it), at least for a time while you collect the evidence. This may seem rather scary. But think of it like this: if, after, say, three months, you remain unconvinced, you can always go back to Theory A and carry on with your current solutions. You might believe that the risk of being seriously ill through

EXERCISE 2.1: THEORY A AND THEORY B

Theory A:

Theory B:

testing out Theory B is too high to take a leap of faith. But if you don't test out theory B, then we can almost certainly say that your symptoms of health anxiety are likely to progress and you won't ever know if you can achieve a much better quality of life. If there's nothing there, you can always go back to your theory; but if you don't test out the alternative Theory B, you will be sticking to your own way of coping, causing yourself more distress and limiting your life even more.

When problematic solutions seem to work

There are two steps in maintaining health anxiety. The first is the way you may be habitually interpreting normal sensations (like dizziness, tiredness) as evidence of a severe illness. As we have seen, this is called 'catastrophizing', and we discuss it in more detail in Chapter 4. Thus you might interpret a headache caused by tension as a brain tumour. Not surprisingly, if you believe this intrusive thought (when it is not true), you will make yourself feel more anxious. Some people experience intrusive thoughts and images about death or severe illness without any obvious trigger. Again, if you habitually view such intrusions as being important in the here and now, then it's not surprising that you will make yourself feel anxious. The second step in understanding how health anxiety is maintained is understanding the way that some your attempts to relieve yourself of anxiety are the very things that are keeping it going.

My solutions are the problem is a phrase we very much want you to keep in mind when you consider what is keeping your health anxiety going. By this we mean that we hope you'll come to understand that the strategies you've come to use to try to reduce your uncertainty and anxiety about your health are fuelling your worry. They are very understandable ways of coping with intrusive thoughts about a health problem.

All the following solutions might appear to work at first in that they reduce anxiety in the short term. Their aim is to increase the feeling of certainty and influence over events. Yet while you may feel that they are working at first, gradually they increase preoccupation and distress. They can produce new sensations, fuel doubt, and increase the sense of feeling out of control.

As time goes by, you may become more depressed. Your friends and family might end up taking on your responsibilities. This in turn creates another feedback loop in which you lose your confidence and feel incapable of doing certain things. You may miss out on meaningful, enjoyable events and opportunities. Avoidance stops you from doing what is important to you. For example, you want to be a person to whom your friends and family can turn for support or you want to be a good mother or father. When you can't do these things you will inevitably feel more depressed. You might spend more time focusing on yourself and beating yourself up and find that you cannot act in a way that is important to you. Your behavior then has an effect on the people around you. Others may be critical or unsupportive and you will probably become more depressed, moving in a vicious circle.

Table 2.1 'The solution is the problem'

WORRY	WAY OF COPING	UNINTENDED CONSEQUENCES
I have AIDS	Getting more information on the Internet	Increases doubt and uncertainty; generates more questions to research
I have stomach cancer	Seeking more medical opinions and investigations	Makes the concern seem more real; increases doubt; generates more false trails; makes me less able to tolerate doubt
I have a brain tumour	Self-reassurance	Increases doubt and uncertainty; generates more questions to research
I'm going to have a heart attack	Reviewing past reassurances	Increases my preoccupation and doubt and makes me less interested in my values
Thoughts of illness and death	Trying to push the thoughts out of my mind	Increases the number of distressing thoughts. Makes them more intrusive and I cannot generate new information
I'm going to die of breast cancer	Try to replace bad thoughts with happy thoughts	Increases the number of distressing thoughts. Makes them more intrusive and I cannot generate new information
I'm going to get a degenerative nerve disease from toxic chemicals	Avoiding or escaping from new or threatening situations or activities	Cannot generate new information; increases my fear of illness; feel more depressed as I come to realize that avoidance does not work

Don't take our word for it

You might well be sceptical about this 'solutions are the problem' idea since naturally you've been trying to help yourself, and much of what you've done is only common sense. Take reassurance, for example. Doctors are in fact trained to give reassurance so it seems reasonable for them to give it and for you to seek it – right? Except that health anxiety by definition is a *preoccupation that persists despite medical reassurance*. This means that it's crucial you try treating your problem as if it's a worry about a health problem rather than an actual or possible health problem.

If you are not convinced that safety behaviors make things worse, try a 'real-life' behavioral experiment.

- Spend one day dealing with your health anxiety the usual way, and record the degree of distress and amount of time you spent in that day preoccupied with your health anxiety.
- Spend the next day increasing the frequency and duration of a safety behavior or double it if you can.
- The following day, go back to your usual way.

Take a look at the results of your three-day experiment. What do you make of them? Most people discover that the harder they try to seek reassurance, or increase their checking, the worse their preoccupation and feelings about their health are.

Putting it together: The vicious flower of health anxiety

We have previously emphasized the importance of identifying the factors that *maintain* the problem and keep it going in a series of vicious circles that aggravate your experience of depression. The vicious flower diagram, with its vicious circles (or 'petals'), is a way of dramatically illustrating to yourself the maintaining factors of your health anxiety. When you draw your vicious flower the aim is to make connections between the way you cope when you feel anxious and the *effect* of the way you cope. The first half of each petal represents an 'output' of health anxiety such as an emotion, a checking behavior, or self-focused attention. The second half is the unintended consequence that follows and feeds back into the maintenance of health anxious preoccupation.

Now use the following blank diagram and draw out your own vicious flower, similar to the example we have given. You can add or modify this as you learn more about your problem. This will give you your own personalized summary of what is keeping your health anxiety going, and therefore show you what to change to reduce your anxiety and preoccupation.

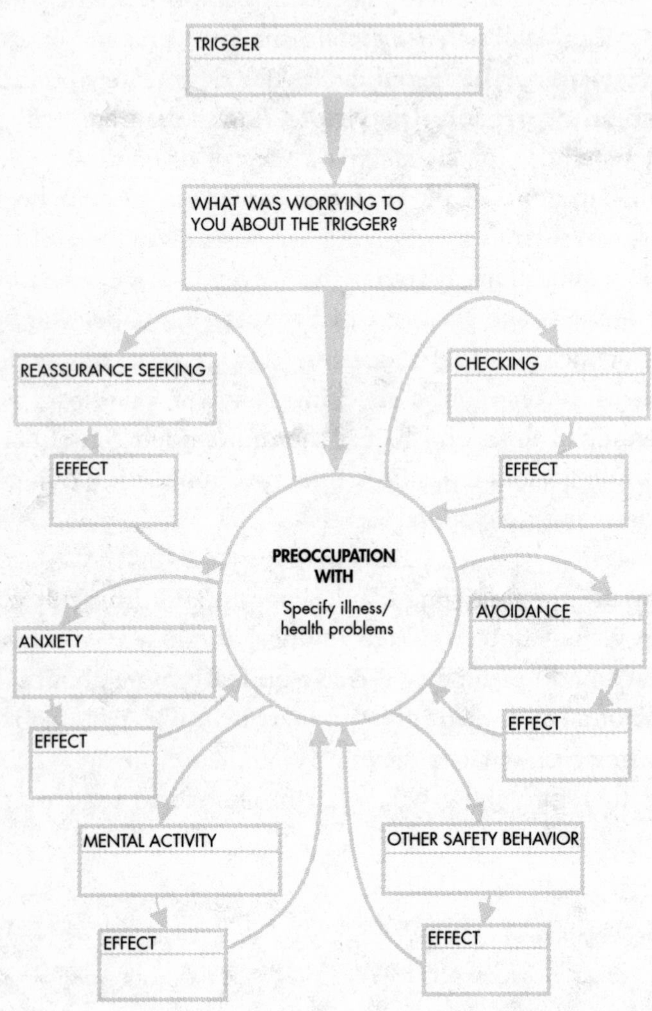
TRIGGER
WHAT WAS WORRYING TO YOU ABOUT THE TRIGGER?
REASSURANCE SEEKING
EFFECT
CHECKING
EFFECT
PREOCCUPATION WITH
Specify illness/ health problems
ANXIETY
EFFECT
AVOIDANCE
EFFECT
MENTAL ACTIVITY
EFFECT
OTHER SAFETY BEHAVIOR
EFFECT

3

Defining your problem, setting goals and finding direction

This chapter is designed to help you define your problem and monitor the severity of your health anxiety and the impact on your life. Identifying and rating the current severity of your health anxiety at the outset will give you a reference point against which you can measure your progress. They are designed to help you define the nature of the problem and effect on your life. Most of the scales can be completed weekly or fortnightly to determine whether you are making progress or not.

THE HEALTH ANXIETY INVENTORY

QUESTIONNAIRE 3.1

Each question consists of a group of four statements. Please read each group of statements carefully and then select the one that best describes your feelings over the past week. Identify the statement by ringing the letter next to it. For example, if you think that statement a) is correct, ring statement a). It may be that more than one statement applies, in which case please ring any that are applicable.

1a) I do not worry about my health.
b) I occasionally worry about my health.
c) I spend much of my time worrying about my health.
d) I spend most of my time worrying about my health.

2a) I notice aches/pains less than most other people (of my age).
b) I notice aches/pains as much as most other people (of my age).
c) I notice aches/pains more than most other people (of my age).
d) I am aware of aches/pains in my body all the time.

3a) As a rule I am not aware of bodily sensations or changes.
b) Sometimes I am aware of bodily sensations or changes.
c) I am often aware of bodily sensations or changes.
d) I am constantly aware of bodily sensations or changes.

4a) Resisting thoughts of illness is never a problem.
b) Most of the time I can resist thoughts of illness.
c) I try to resist thoughts of illness but am often unable to do so.
d) Thoughts of illness are so strong that I no longer even try to resist them.

5a) As a rule I am not afraid that I have a serious illness.
b) I am sometimes afraid that I have a serious illness.
c) I am often afraid that I have a serious illness.
d) I am always afraid that I have a serious illness.

6a) I do not have images (mental pictures) of myself being ill.
b) I occasionally have images of myself being ill.
c) I frequently have images of myself being ill.
d) I constantly have images of myself being ill.

7a) I do not have any difficulty taking my mind off thoughts about my health.
b) I sometimes have difficulty taking my mind off thoughts about my health.
c) I often have difficulty in taking my mind off thoughts about my health.
d) Nothing can take my mind off thoughts about my health.

8a) I am lastingly relieved if my doctor tells me there is nothing wrong.
b) I am initially relieved but the worries sometimes return later.
c) I am initially relieved but the worries always return later.
d) I am not relieved if my doctor tells me there is nothing wrong.

9a) If I hear about an illness I never think I have it myself.
b) If I hear about an illness I sometimes think I have it myself.
c) If I hear about an illness I often think I have it myself.
d) If I hear about an illness I always think I have it myself.

10a) If I have a bodily sensation or change I rarely wonder what it means.
b) If I have a bodily sensation or change I often wonder what it means.

c) If I have a bodily sensation or change I always wonder what it means.
d) If I have a bodily sensation or change I must know what it means.

11a) I usually feel at very low risk of developing a serious illness.
b) I usually feel at fairly low risk of developing a serious illness.
c) I usually feel at moderate risk of developing a serious illness.
d) I usually feel at high risk of developing a serious illness.

12a) I never think I have a serious illness.
b) I sometimes think I have a serious illness.
c) I often think I have a serious illness.
d) I usually think that I am seriously ill.

13a) If I notice an unexplained bodily sensation I don't find it difficult to think about other things.
b) If I notice an unexplained bodily sensation I sometimes find it difficult to think about other things.
c) If I notice an unexplained bodily sensation I often find it difficult to think about other things.
d) If I notice an unexplained bodily sensation I always find it difficult to think about other things.

14a) My family/friends would say I do not worry enough about my health.

b) My family/friends would say I have a normal attitude to my health.
c) My family/friends would say I worry too much about my health.
d) My family/friends would say I am a hypochondriac.

Score 0 for items circled a), score 1 for items circled b), 2 for items circled c), 3 for items circled d). If you score 18 or more, you probably have health anxiety and may benefit from an assessment by a health professional. You can also use the scale to measure your progress in a self-help program, your work with a therapist or use of medication for health anxiety.

Source: This questionnaire is reproduced with permission from the main author. It was developed by P. Salkovskis, K. Rimes, H. Warwick and D. M. Clark, (2002), 'The health anxiety inventory: development and validation of scales for the measurement of health anxiety and hypochondriasis', in *Psychological Medicine*, 32, 843–53.

Rating the impact of your health anxiety on your life

People's problems sometimes affect their ability to do certain day-to-day tasks in their lives. To rate your problems with health anxiety look at each numbered section in Exercise 3.1 below and determine on the scale provided how much your problem impairs your ability to carry out the activity.

EXERCISE 3.1. WORK AND SOCIAL FUNCTIONING

1 **WORK OR STUDY** To what extent does your health anxiety interfere in your ability to work or study? (If you are retired or choose not to have a job for reasons unrelated to your problem, please tick N/A (not applicable).

0	1	2	3	4	5	6	7	8	N/A
Not at all		Slightly		Definitely		Markedly		Very severely, I cannot work	☐

2 **HOME MANAGEMENT** To what extent does your health anxiety interfere in your home management (e.g. cleaning, tidying, shopping, cooking, looking after home/children, paying bills, etc)?

0	1	2	3	4	5	6	7	8	N/A
Not at all		Slightly		Definitely		Markedly		Very severely	☐

3 **SOCIAL LEISURE ACTIVITIES** To what extent does your health anxiety interfere in your social life with other people (e.g. parties, pubs, outings, entertaining, etc.)?

0	1	2	3	4	5	6	7	8	N/A
Not at all		Slightly		Definitely		Markedly		Very severely	☐

4 **PRIVATE LEISURE ACTIVITIES** To what extent does your health anxiety interfere in your private leisure activities done alone (e.g. reading, gardening, sewing, hobbies, walking, etc.)?

0	1	2	3	4	5	6	7	8	N/A
Not at all		Slightly		Definitely		Markedly		Very severely	☐

5 **FAMILY AND RELATIONSHIPS** To what extent does your health anxiety interfere in your ability to form and maintain close relationships with others including the people whom you live with?

0	1	2	3	4	5	6	7	8	N/A
Not at all		Slightly		Definitely		Markedly		Very severely	☐

6 **EFFECT ON HEALTH** To what extent does your health anxiety make you physically unhealthy? (For example you smoke more, you give up exercising, you neglect your eating; checking and rubbing your skin causes inflammation.)

0	1	2	3	4	5	6	7	8	N/A
Not at all		Slightly		Definitely		Markedly		Very severely	☐

TOTAL OF 6 ITEMS =

Defining your problems

Coming up with a list of your problems helps in a number of ways. First it helps you to break down your health anxiety into specific areas to tackle. It also gives you a chance to rate these problems now, overall, so that you can re-rate them later and so measure your progress.

SAMPLE PROBLEM LIST

Severity rating: 0–10 (Where 0 is no problem and 10 very severe)

1 Being very worried with a fear that I might develop cancer, leading me to think about it most of the day, and repeatedly check my body and seek reassurance

Rating: 10

2 Feeling depressed, leading me to spend as much time as I can at home and not keeping on top of my bills and avoiding seeing my friends or doing any chores.

Rating: 8

Now make your own list of problems and rate the severity of each one.

EXERCISE 3.2: PROBLEM LIST

Severity rating: 0–10 (Where 0 is no problem and 10 is very severe)

1 ______________________________

____

Rating: ____________

2 ______________________________

____

Rating: ____________

3 ______________________________

____

Rating: ____________

4 ______________________________

____

Rating: ____________

Describing your goals

Next, you need to write a description of your goals relating to the problems that you have described and the values you have identified. Start with short-term goals, which are easier to tackle, and set yourself a realistic timetable by which you intend to move on to the next set of goals.

SAMPLE GOAL LIST

Progress rating: 0–10 (Where 0 = no progress and 10 = total improvement)

Goals	Progress rating
Short term	
1 To stop repeatedly checking my body and instead get to work on time	1
2 To stop investigating symptoms on the Internet and instead spend at last an hour a day with my children.	8
Medium term	
1 To resume my social life by meeting up with friends outside my home twice a week	3
2 To go to the gym three times a week	5
3 To go out to local shopping centre once a week	5
Long term	
1 To be a good partner and spend time doing things together	3
2 To learn to play the piano and practise daily	4

Try to make your own goals as specific, observable and realistic as possible.

Some individuals with health anxiety have forgotten what is normal or healthy. To help generate ideas for healthy alternative behaviors, consider the following questions:

- What did you do before you had a health anxiety?
- If you had a twin, who was the same as you in every respect but without health anxiety, what would they do?
- What would a role model of yours do?
- What would someone who inspires you do?

You will need to ask yourself these questions for goals in the short, medium and long term. You can then monitor your progress towards your goals on a scale of zero to 10, where zero is no progress at all towards the goal and 10 means the goal has been achieved and sustained. Remember to make sure that your goals relate to your valued directions in life and tackle what you have been avoiding.

EXERCISE 3.3: LIST OF GOALS

Progress rating: 0–10 (Where 0 = no progress and 10 = goal completely reached)

Short term

1 ______________________ ☐

2 ______________________ ☐

3 ______________________ ☐

Medium term

1 ______________________ ☐

2 ______________________ ☐

3 ______________________ ☐

Long term

1 ______________________ ☐

2 ______________________ ☐

3 ______________________ ☐

Focusing more on what's important to you, and less on health

Much of health anxiety is the result of becoming overly focused on:

- your own health
- other people's health
- health in the media, or
- the place of health, illness and death in our culture.

The aim of the next exercise is to gain an understanding of your values or what you want your life to stand for. This will enable you to engage in a life that has a better balance and is less dominated by health. Once you know what your valued directions are, you can start moving towards them. To help you monitor whether you are in fact acting according to your values, we have prepared various tables and exercises for you to work through. There are various prompts for each area where you can write down a brief statement. You don't have to fill in a values statement for every area; just leave an area blank if you think it is inappropriate for you. After writing down your statements, you may want to clarify them with a friend or therapist. Be careful not to write down values that you think you should have just because others will approve of them. Only write down what you know to be true for yourself. It is probably a valued direction if you acted on it consistently before you experienced your health anxiety. If you have had a health anxiety for many years, you may struggle with this exercise, but you should persevere because it is very important.

Note that values are not goals – they are more like compass points and they need to be lived out through committed action. Goals are part of the process of committing yourself to action. Goals are achievable – for example, you can get married, which is one goal – whereas values are more open-ended: with values, you never reach your destination because there is always something more you can do to work towards them, such as being a good partner. If your valued direction in life is to be a good parent, then your first goal might be to spend a few hours just hanging out with your son or daughter and playing with him or her. Other goals might be to get your son or daughter through school or college as part of the valued direction of being a good parent. This does not mean you will not fail at times – it means that if and when you fail, you can learn from it, take responsibility and restart your commitment to the action. It might take some time to discover all your values, so here are some prompts to help you:

- Imagine what aspects of life you would be engaging in if you were not feeling anxious or preoccupied with your health at this moment. We understand that you may feel upset at the things you seem to have lost, but this exercise will help you chart your course on the journey you wish to take.

- Brainstorm all the activities and interests you can think of, and consider which might be close to your valued directions.
- Remind yourself of what you used to value or aspire to when you were younger. Have any of these values simply been 'squashed' by your health anxiety?
- Consider whether a fear of what other people will think, or a fear of failing, might be holding you back from pursuing your valued directions.
- Consider a role model or hero and the values he or she holds.
- Have a chat with a trusted friend (or therapist) who knows you well and see what he or she would guess your values to be.
- Be prepared to experiment and 'try on for size', living consistently with a given valued direction to see how it 'fits'.

SAMPLE VALUED DIRECTIONS FORM

Area	Valued direction
1 Intimacy (What is important to you in how you act in an intimate relationship? What sort of partner do you want to be? If you are not involved in a relationship at present, how would you like to act in a relationship?)	*I want to develop a relationship and be a good partner and spend time doing things together.*
2 Family relationships (What is important to you in how you want to act as a brother/sister; son/daughter; father/mother or parent-in-law? If you are not in contact with some of your family members, would you like to be and how would you act in such a relationship?)	*I'd like to be a good daughter and less dependent on my parents for support and to help them more in the future. I'd like to spend more time with my brother, getting to know him better.*
3 Social relationships (What is important to you in the way you act in the friendships you have? How would you like your friends to remember you? If you have no friends, would you like to have some and what role would you like in a friendship?)	*I'd like to be a good friend, more open and available to my friends.*
4 Work (What is important to you in your work? What sort of employee do you want to be? How important to you is what you achieve in your career? What sort of business do you want to run?)	*I'd like to return to work and be more approachable and help to make it a more successful company.*
5 Education and training (What is important to you in your education or training? What sort of student do you want to be? If you are not in education, would you like to be?)	*To improve my future prospects of securing a better job in the future, I'd like to do more management and IT training.*

Area	Valued direction
6 Recreation (What is important to you in what you do to follow any interests, sports or hobbies? If you are not following any interests, what would you ideally like to be pursuing?)	*I'd like to get back to playing tennis and swimming. I might like to learn to play a musical instrument.*
7 Spirituality (If you are spiritual, what is important to you in the way you want to follow a spiritual path? If you are not, would you like to be and what do you ideally want?)	*I'd like to learn more about Buddhism.*
8 Voluntary work (What would you like to do for the larger community? For example, voluntary or charity work or political activity?)	*I'd like to do more to help others in a charity for health anxiety or for obsessive compulsive disorder and raise money for them.*
9 Health/physical well-being (What is important to you in how you act for your physical health?)	*Eating a healthy diet and taking exercise.*
10 Mental health (What is important to you generally in how you look after your mental health?)	*I'd like to be better at managing my stress at the end of the working day.*

Now try to define your own valued directions in life.

EXERCISE 3.4: UNDERSTANDING YOUR VALUES

Area	Valued direction
1 Intimacy (What is important to you in how you act in an intimate relationship? What sort of partner do you want to be? If you are not involved in a relationship at present, how would you like to act in a relationship?)	
2 Family relationships (What is important to you in how you want to act as a brother/sister; son/daughter; father/mother or parent-in-law? If you are not in contact with some of your family members, would you like to be and how would you act in such a relationship?)	
3 Social relationships (What is important to you in the way you act in the friendships you have? How would you like your friends to remember you? If you have no friends, would you like to have some and what role would you like in a friendship?)	
4 Work (What is important to you in your work? What sort of employee do you want to be? How important to you is what you achieve in your career? What sort of business do you want to run?)	

Area	Valued direction
5 Education and training (What is important to you in your education or training? What sort of student do you want to be? If you are not in education, would you like to be?)	
6 Recreation (What is important to you in what you do to follow any interests, sports or hobbies? If you are not following any interests, what would you ideally like to be pursuing?)	
7 Spirituality (If you are spiritual, what is important to you in the way you want to follow a spiritual path? If you are not, would you like to be and what do you ideally want?)	
8 Voluntary work (What would you like to do for the larger community? For example, voluntary or charity work or political activity?)	
9 Health/physical well-being (What is important to you in how you act for your physical health?)	

Area	Valued direction
9 Health/physical well-being (What is important to you in how you act for your physical health?)	
10 Mental health (What is important to you generally in how you look after your mental health?)	
11 Any other values that are not listed above	

Source: Adapted from the 'Valued Living Questionnaire', *Acceptance and Commitment Therapy* (Guilford Publications, 2004) by Steven Hayes, Kirk Strosahl and Kelly Wilson.

4

Dealing with anxiety-provoking thoughts and images

As we described in Chapter 1, when you feel anxious, worried and preoccupied about the idea that you have a medical problem you may experience both thoughts and images related to your concern. This chapter is about developing a different relationship with your thoughts and images so you can treat them as 'just thoughts' or 'just a picture in my mind'. Your life will be more rewarding when you truly accept your thoughts and images about your health as just thoughts; whereas trying to 'control' them only makes the worry worse and amplifies your discomfort into pain. This chapter also contains a number of practical exercises to help you examine your relationship with your thoughts.

Thought suppression

One way of not experiencing unpleasant thoughts or images is to try to suppress them. This often occurs when people have experienced an unpleasant event like a death or a trauma. However, suppressing thoughts will also bring unintended consequences; it has the effect of increasing the frequency of those thoughts, making you feel worse – trying not to think of something increases rather than decreases its intrusiveness. Try the following exercise.

EXERCISE 4.1: THOUGHT SUPPRESSION ILLUSTRATION

The pink elephant experiment

Close your eyes and imagine a pink elephant. Now try really hard not to think of pink elephants for a minute, try to push any images of pink elephants out of your mind.

What did you notice was the effect of trying not to think of pink elephants?

Most people who do this exercise find that all they can think of is pink elephants. In research, this effect is called the 'white bear effect', from studies showing that when participants were asked to not to think of white bears, they had more thoughts about them. Understanding the apparent upside down way in which the human mind works is a key to understanding and overcoming health anxiety. Very many people with this problem are caught in the trap of trying too hard to rid themselves of thoughts and doubts, and in fact this brings about the very opposite of what they want. Still not convinced that trying to get rid of intrusive thoughts, images, or doubts makes them worse?
Try a more 'real life' experiment.

EXERCISE 4.2: REAL LIFE THOUGHT SUPPRESSION EXPERIMENT

a) Spend one day dealing with your thoughts in the usual way, and record their frequency and the distress they cause you.
b) Spend the next day trying even harder to get rid of your thoughts and record their frequency and the distress they cause you. Try as hard as you can to suppress them. (c) The following day go back to your usual way of dealing with your negative thoughts, and then the next day return to step (b).

Take a look at the results of your four-day experiment. What do you make of them? Most people discover that their thoughts become more frequent and disturbing the harder they try to get rid of them. Stop trying so hard not have the thought or image that's bothering you and it will bother you much less! After all, a thought is only intrusive if you don't let it in and recognize it for what it is. Embrace such thoughts and fully accept them and you will carry them as part of you.

Label your thinking style

You may have forgotten how to observe the process of thinking because you have become bound up with the content of your thoughts. The first step is to thank your mind for its contribution to your mental health. Try to distance yourself from its endless chatter and commentary and rating of yourself. This is a difficult skill, which will take time and practice to master, using a number of different exercises (described below).

Just as having an infection might give you a fever, emotional problems will affect your thinking. In common with other emotional problems, health anxiety will drive your thinking in a negative and extreme direction. This unhelpful way of thinking will in turn make you feel worse, and influence what you focus upon and what you do. It thus plays a key role in maintaining your problem.

Two of the founding fathers of cognitive behavior therapy, Albert Ellis and Aaron Beck, both identified particular patterns of thinking linked with emotional problems. The great advantage of knowing the ways in which your thinking might be affected by our health anxiety is that you can more readily spot a negative thought and learn to take these thoughts (and images) with a huge pinch of salt. Think of it as health anxiety propaganda, aiming to keep you preoccupied and distressed. Just as people during the Second World War had to learn to ignore Nazi propaganda (aimed at lowering their morale) that invaded their radios, so you can learn to notice unhelpful thoughts without believing them to be true.

Health anxiety thinking styles

Here are some of the more common types of thinking styles that arise in health anxiety.

Catastrophizing

Jumping to the worst possible conclusion. For example:

heart skipping a beat	*I'm going to have a heart attack*
lumps under the skin	*I've got cancer*
tingling or numbness	*I've got Multiple Sclerosis*
headache	*I've got a brain tumour*
feeling run down	*I'm dying*

All-or-nothing (black-or-white) thinking

Thinking in extreme, all-or-nothing terms. For example: 'I am either totally free from disease' or 'I am ill and will soon experience a slow painful death.'

Over-generalizing

Drawing generalized conclusions often (involving the words 'always' or 'never') from a specific event. For example: 'Because I've worried for a long time I'll never be free from it.'

Fortune-telling

Making negative and pessimistic predictions about the future. For example: 'I know I'll never get over this. I'm bound to end up dying alone. It's inevitable that my children will be terribly distressed for the rest of their lives if I die and leave them without a father/mother.'

Mind reading

Jumping to conclusions about what other people are thinking about you. For example: 'my doctor didn't look me in the eye because he knows there is something seriously wrong with me.'

Mental filtering

Focusing on the negative and overlooking the positive. For example: focusing upon your vulnerability to illness or tending to pay more attention to the tiny amount of evidence that supports your worry.

Disqualifying the positive

Discounting positive information or twisting a positive into a negative. For example: 'The doctor said I was fine, but I think he may have been tired and not concentrating properly. There's no point in enjoying life if you know that one day you'll die.'

Labelling

Globally defining yourself. For example: 'I'm vulnerable in my health, I'm fragile, I'm defective.'

Emotional reasoning

Listening too much to your negative gut feeling instead of looking at the objective facts. For example: 'I know there's something wrong with me, I can just feel it. There must be something wrong otherwise I wouldn't feel so anxious.'

Personalizing

Taking an event or someone's behavior too personally. For example: 'the way the newsagent looked at me when he handed my magazine was because he knows I'm ill.'

Demands

Rigid 'should', 'must', 'ought', or 'have to' rules about myself, the world, or other people. Demands for certainty can be a particular issue for any kind of anxiety problem. For example: 'I must know whether there is anything wrong with my body so that I can do whatever I can about it.'

Low frustration tolerance

Telling yourself that something is 'too difficult', or 'unbearable', or saying that 'I can't stand it', when it's actually hard to bear, but bearable. It is in your interests to tolerate these things and to experience some degree of discomfort as you face your fears.

EXERCISE 4.3: IDENTIFYING YOUR COMMON THINKING STYLES

Write down examples of your five most common thinking styles.

1 Thinking style ______________________

Example ______________________

____

2 Thinking style ______________________

Example ______________________

____

3 Thinking style ______________________

Example ______________________

____

4 Thinking style ______________________

Example ______________________

____

5 Thinking style ______________________

Example ______________________

____

Labelling your thoughts and feelings

Another strategy for intrusive thoughts is to label the thought or feeling by saying it out aloud and writing it down. This can be helpful to stop confusing the thoughts about illness with facts. For example:

I am ***having a thought*** *that I am ill.*
I am ***having a memory*** *of being in hospital as a child.*
I'm ***having the feeling*** *of being anxious.*
I'm ***making a rating*** *of myself that I am vulnerable in my health.*

As an alternative, some people find it more helpful to distance themselves from such thoughts by labelling them as products of their mind. For example: 'My mind is telling me I am ill.'

EXERCISE 4.4: LABELLING YOUR HABITUAL THOUGHTS

Now try to complete the following for your own habitual pattern of thoughts and feelings:

I am having a thought that (describe)

I am having a thought that (describe)

I am having a feeling of (describe)

I am having memories about (describe)

I am making a rating about (describe)

Labelling your thoughts may feel awkward at first, but with practice it will help you to accept your thoughts or feelings without 'buying into' them. Some people find it helpful to speak their thoughts out loud in a funny voice or in the voice of a cartoon character. Again, this can help you to distance yourself from your thoughts and defuse them from your 'self'.

The aim of all these exercises is to acknowledge the existence of such thoughts and label them for what they are. As you progress, you'll discover that you can experience unpleasant thoughts and feelings and still do what's important for your life, despite their presence. If you keep doing this, they will slowly fade away.

Keeping a record of your thoughts

Try making a list of all your recurrent body image thoughts and feelings, label them for what they are, and put a tick in the relevant box below each time they occur. Such thoughts are more likely to appear in difficult situations. It can be helpful to monitor them just to see which ones turn up in particular situations and try to 'bully you'. We don't want you to do this repeatedly – just to see what happens over a few days. You will soon start to develop different ways of looking at your thoughts rather than buying into them or paying attention to what your mind is telling you. An example is shown overleaf:

SAMPLE THOUGHT-MONITORING CHART

	Mon	Tues	Wed	Thurs	Fri	Sat	Sun
I have thoughts that I'll find out that I'm ill	✓✓ ✓✓ ✓✓ ✓✓ ✓	✓✓ ✓✓ ✓✓	✓✓ ✓✓ ✓✓✓ ✓✓ ✓✓	✓✓ ✓✓ ✓✓			
I have a thought that I'm going to die	✓✓ ✓✓ ✓✓ ✓✓	✓✓ ✓✓ ✓✓ ✓✓✓	✓✓ ✓✓ ✓✓ ✓✓	✓✓ ✓✓ ✓✓			
I have images of myself lying in bed in hospital	✓✓ ✓✓ ✓✓ ✓✓	✓✓ ✓✓ ✓✓	✓✓ ✓✓ ✓✓ ✓	✓✓ ✓✓ ✓✓			

A blank thought-monitoring chart can be found on the next page, and in Appendix 3 (page 293), which you can photocopy. Note that the purpose of monitoring your thoughts is not to challenge their content, or to control or reduce their frequency – just to acknowledge them, note the thinking error and to thank your mind for its contribution. If your thoughts are very frequent (and in some people they may occur 1,000 or more times a day) you might find it easier to use a tally counter and transfer the total at the end of each day to your chart. (You can purchase a tally counter by post. You will easily find a supplier if you type 'buy tally counter' into an Internet search engine.) You can also note the situations in which the thoughts most commonly occur in order to see if there is a pattern. It would be useful to know if there is such a pattern so that you can predict what thoughts will turn up and ensure that you are better prepared for them.

EXERCISE 4.5: THOUGHT-MONITORING CHART

In the left-hand column note your most common intrusive thoughts and images about your appearance, and then tick the relevant column (Mon–Sun) each time you have that thought, or add the total from your tally counter.

	Mon	Tues	Wed	Thurs	Fri	Sat	Sun
I have an intrusive thought that							
I have an intrusive thought that							
I have an intrusive thought that							

I have an intrusive thought that							
I have an intrusive thought image of							
I have an intrusive image of							

De-catastrophizing 1: Understanding some of the bodily and mental sensations that are caused by anxiety

Something that can be very helpful in overcoming catastrophic misinterpretations of bodily or mental sensations is to understand that they may have an alternative explanation – for example, that they are consequences of anxiety. This has two advantages:

It's a less scary interpretation of what's going on;

It gives you a clear plan for what to change – reducing your anxiety using the techniques we've outlined in this book – rather than checking or seeking reassurance.

There are an enormous number of physical and mental 'outputs' of anxiety, some of which are incredibly powerful. Its therefore easy to see how they could be misinterpreted as a sign of something being wrong, when in fact they are a sign of your body's fight-or-flight anxiety response being in very good working order. The diagram below illustrates some of the more common mental and physical sensations driven by anxiety.

Figure 4.1 Diagram of body with anxiety symptoms

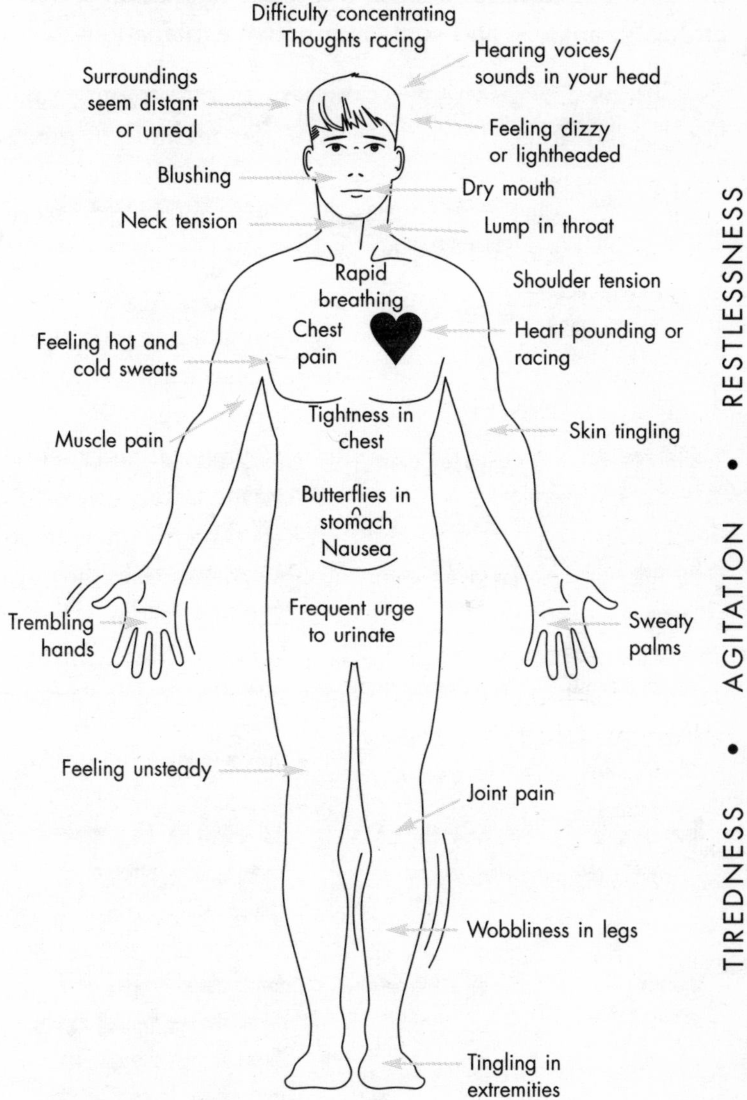

In Table 4.1 below are some examples of body sensations, the kind of catastrophic misinterpretations that are driven by health anxiety, and some alternative explanations.

TABLE 4.1: EXAMPLES OF BODY SENSATIONS AND POSSIBLE EXPLANATIONS

Body sensation	Catastrophic misinterpretation	Possible alternative explanation
Joint pain	My bones are wearing out	Some stiffness in joints is completely normal, especially after exercise or inactivity
Ache in my leg	I've got bone cancer	Muscle tension or a strained muscle
Red marks on my skin	I've got skin cancer	A scratch, having knocked against something, an insect bite
Stomach cramps	I've got stomach cancer	Gastric discomfort caused by acid entering your stomach due to stress or anxiety
Heart racing	My overworking heart will be getting worn out	Raised heart rate due to adrenalin caused by stress, anxiety or caffeine
Headache	I've got a brain tumour	Tension created by tightening of the muscles over the skull; may be caused by stress or anxiety, too much caffeine, hangover from too much alcohol, or lack of sleep

I can feel a sore patch on my mouth	I've got mouth cancer	A mouth ulcer, a burn from hot food, a scratch from food or toothbrush, having accidentally bitten part of your mouth
Chest pain	I've got a heart problem	Tension in the muscles between your ribs caused by stress or anxiety
Feeling tired all the time	I've got a cancer of the blood cells	Fatigue caused by anxiety, fatigued driven by low mood, being restless and not sleeping well
My surroundings feel distant and unreal	I'm losing touch with reality, I'm going to develop schizophrenia	Being tired, anxiety causing 'derealization' (a natural protection against stressful events)
Tingling sensations in my hands	I've got Multiple Sclerosis	Too much oxygen in your blood caused by over-breathing when feeling anxious or stressed.
My breasts feel tender	I've got breast cancer	Swelling and tenderness caused by hormonal changes in menstrual cycle, ill fitting bra, accidental bruising, bruising caused by excessive checking

In summary, there is every chance that there is an alternative explanation for your experience of body sensations. Consider the following possibilities:

- It's a normal physical sensation that you are focusing upon and is therefore 'amplified' in your awareness, but normally would not be on your mind.
- It's the physical result of your emotions such as anxiety, stress, or depression. Again these can be amplified if you focus upon them.
- It's the result of minor physical ailment.
- It's a benign 'Medically Unexplained Physical Symptom' (see Chapter 1).

You can use the chart opposite to develop your own, less anxiety-provoking interpretations of the body sensations you tend to worry about.

Remember not all sensations have a clear explanation, so you might need to take the practical, self-helping decision to assume they are not the product of a disease unless proven otherwise. In the UK recently, advertisement posters with the slogan 'Doubt Kills' promoted awareness of heart disease. This of course was aimed at people who are *not concerned enough* about their health (and almost certainly won't be reading this book!). But this is an uncertain universe, and it's important to remember that doubt is normal and it's healthy for our minds to be able to tolerate doubt – so look for probable explanations, not certain ones.

EXERCISE 4.6: ALTERNATIVE EXPLANATIONS

Body sensation	Catastrophic misinterpretation	Possible alternative explanation

De-catastrophizing 2: Conducting a survey to normalize bodily and mental sensations

Describe the problem

I'm worried that when I can't stop my mind racing this is a sign that I might develop schizophrenia, and even though I've seen three doctors I can't be convinced that there's nothing wrong with me.

Identify the prediction you want to test

That other people don't get such strong feelings that they cant stop their mind racing, which means there must be something physically wrong with my mind.

Formulate an alternative prediction

That some people might also have strong mental sensations, especially when they feel anxious or stressed.

Specify how you will test your prediction

I'll conduct a survey of people I know and ask whether they have ever felt their thoughts racing or as if they can't get their mind under control.

Write down the results of your experiment

I spoke to nine people. All could relate to times when they 'feel as if they are going crazy' especially when they feel really stressed and things are getting on top of them.

Analyse the results of your experiment

It seems my mental experience is very normal, especially at times of stress. I suppose that my fear of going mad is leading me to notice these sensations more, and to have them more because I'm so stressed by my fear of going mad!

Now try your own experiment.

EXERCISE 4.7: DESCRIBE THE PROBLEM

Identify the prediction you want to test

Formulate an alternative prediction

Specify how you will test your prediction

Write down the results of your experiment

____

____

____

Analyse the results of your experiment

____

____

____

Have you learned anything from your experiment? Consider whether another experiment might be helpful.

De-catastrophizing 3: Not being sure, but treating your problem 'as if' it's anxiety anyway

Trying to be certain about whether your body or mental sensations are a sign of actual or pending disease is part of the problem, not part of the solution. Assuming you've been reassured by a doctor that you are excessively concerned and that, to date, treating your problem as if the problem itself is a disease you are preoccupied with has not helped, your next best step is to try out treating the problem differently. That is, you should try treating your physical sensations and intrusive thoughts and images 'as if' you have a problem with worry about your health (rather than a physical illness). This means using the approach we outline in this book for several weeks, and then stepping back to see the results. If things have improved then that's further confirmation that your problem is primarily one of worry. If they have not improved you can reconsider whether you have been targeting your main unhelpful and coping strategies and try again. You can of course even ultimately return to treating your problem as if it is a physical illness problem and see if this provides a more effective solution.

De-catastrophizing 4: Correcting your psychological bias

Imagine riding a bicycle that tends to veer to the right when you point the handlebars straight ahead. What would you do to make the bicycle go straight (before you had a chance to fix it)? You would correct for the bias towards the right by steering slightly towards the left. You can do exactly the same in your mind: so, if you know that you tend to over-assume illness or danger, you can correct your thinking by deliberately assuming things are ok.

Excessive responsibility and blame

As with other problems such as obsessive compulsive disorder, you may say to yourself, 'I should do all I can to prevent myself from getting ill otherwise if I do become ill it will be all my fault.'

Here's a technique that might bring memories of being taught percentages and fractions at school. You can use a visual method to see more clearly your personal responsibility.

PERSONAL RESPONSIBLITY

1 Think of a health problem you believe you can influence. If this example did happen, how responsible on a 0–100 per cent scale would you estimate yourself to be? The chances are you'll have given yourself a pretty high percentage (if not 100 per cent).
2 List all other possible contributing factors to this feared event, placing your role at the bottom of the list.
3 Draw a circle (your 'pie') and begin to divide up the pie amongst the various contributing factors, giving each a rough percentage and leaving yourself until the very last.
4 Step back and consider the new percentage of responsibility you will have given yourself. Obviously a desired outcome, and the most likely we hope, is for you to experience a degree of relief now that you realize you do not carry sole responsibility for your health.

The aim is not to be 100 per cent medically accurate, but to help your mind see more clearly that you do not have to take such a large amount of responsibility.

See the example on the page overleaf:

Figure 4.2 Responsibility pie chart

THE FEARED OUTCOME THAT I AM PREOCCUPIED WITH THAT I MIGHT DIE PAINFULLY FROM BOWEL CANCER AS A RESULT OF MISSING AN IMPORTANT SYMPTOM

Possible contributing factors:

- My genetics
- Lifestyle factors
- My partner not noticing changes
- My doctor not detecting the problem and his treatment
- Me missing something because I reduce my checking and vigilance

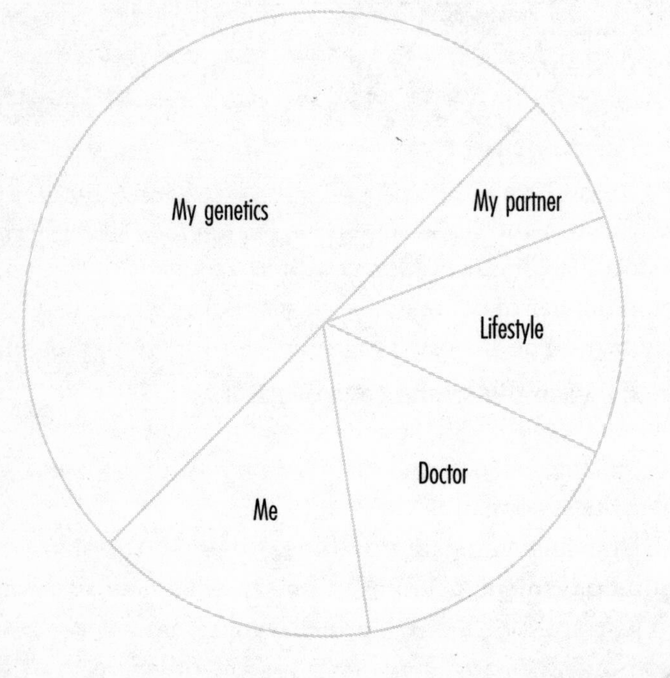

Watching your thoughts pass by

You have gathered by now that what we want you to develop is a sense of distance from your thoughts and feelings. This means not buying into them but being aware of them as a passive observer.

This is best illustrated by closing your eyes and bringing to mind, say, a bowl of fruit, then watching it without influencing it in any way. It's okay if your attention strays away from the orange or if the image changes (for example, the orange falls off the top of the bowl). You should merely be aware of the changing content of your attention without influencing the content in any way. This may not be easy at first, but it's worth persevering. The technique of distancing your thoughts can also be used simply to notice your intrusive thoughts and not to engage with them.

Another analogy for watching your thoughts is to imagine them as cars passing on a road. When you are depressed, you might focus on particular 'cars' that tell you that you are a failure and life is hopeless. You cope either by trying to stop the cars or by pushing them to one side (if you're not in danger of being run over, that is!). Alternatively, you may try to flag the car down, get into the driving seat and try to park it (that is, analyse the idea and sort it out until you feel 'right'). Of course, there is often no room to park the car and as soon as you have parked one car another one comes along.

Distancing yourself from your thoughts means being on the pavement, acknowledging the cars and the traffic but just noticing them and then walking along the pavement and focusing your attention on other parts of the environment (such as talking to the person beside you and noticing other people passing you and the sights and smells of the flowers on the verge). You can still 'play in the park' and do what is important for you despite the thoughts. In other words, such thoughts have no more

EXERCISE 4.8: AN EXERCISE IN DISTANCING

In this exercise, you will need to get into a relaxed position and just observe the flow of your thoughts, one after another, without trying to work out their meaning or their relationship to one another. You are practising an attitude of acceptance of your experience.

Imagine for the moment sitting next to a stream. As you gaze at the stream, you notice a number of leaves on the surface of the water. Keep looking at the leaves and watch them drift slowly downstream. When thoughts come, put each one on a leaf, and notice each leaf as it comes closer to you. Then watch it slowly moving away from you, eventually drifting out of sight. Return to looking at the stream, waiting for the next leaf to float by with a new thought. If one comes along, again, watch it come closer to you and then let it drift out of sight. Allow yourself to have thoughts and imagine them floating by like leaves down a stream. Notice now that you are the stream. You hold all the water, all the fish and debris and leaves. You need not interfere with anything in the stream — just let them all flow. Then, when you are ready, gradually widen your attention to take in the sounds around you. Slowly open your eyes and get back to life.

meaning than passing traffic – they are 'just' thoughts and are part of the rich tapestry of human existence. You can't get rid of them. It's just the same as when you are in a city and there is always some slight traffic noise in the background and you learn to live with it. Notice these thoughts and feelings and acknowledge their presence, then get on with your life.

5

Understanding the process of worrying about your health

One way of looking at health anxiety is to think of it as something that you *do* rather than something that you *suffer from*. You natural question in response might well be 'why would I do this to myself?!' One of the dilemmas in overcoming health anxiety can be that you might, to some extent at least, think it is perfectly reasonable to worry about your health. This idea alone could contribute to years of needless distress, preoccupation and interference in your life. Let's be clear: an appropriate degree of concern and sensible health behaviors is a very long way from the kind of excessive worry that health anxiety involves.

Understand your worry

We understand how difficult it is to stop worrying and how powerful your thoughts can be when they are pulled by emotions. However, we are now going to show you ways in which you can begin to escape the power of worrying. The first step in understanding worrying is to analyse the process. We are going to show you how to understand when you worry and what happens when you worry in order to work out what keeps it going. Your eventual goal will be to stop engaging in the content of your worries.

If your worrying helps you to achieve what you want (and please write to us with some examples), then you can stop at this chapter! If, however, it makes you feel worse or causes you to become inactive or to do something else that is unhelpful, then read on. If you are not sure whether your worrying is helpful, keep a record of its frequency over the next few days, using the chart below, and complete the analysis. If you are still not sure, try to alternate a period (e.g. one day) of worrying extra hard with equal periods of not worrying at all and note the effect on your mood and what you avoid.

EXERCISE 5.1: THE A, B, C OF WORRYING

Activating Event

Describe a recent typical situation in which you were worrying. Did it start with an intrusive thought, image or memory? Did you misinterpret the sensation as evidence of a catastrophe like cancer? What were you doing at the time?

____

____

____

Behavior (what you did in your mind)

What did you tell yourself? Was it a 'what if'? Were you trying to solve a catastrophic thought?

Immediate Consequences

Was there any pay-off from worrying? For example, did you feel as if you were doing something to stop yourself from becoming ill or make the future a bit more certain? Did it mean you didn't have to experience the thought or image of yourself becoming ill?

Unintended Consequences

What effect did the worrying have on the way you felt?

Did worry increase the amount of intrusive thoughts or images about your health?

What effect did worrying have on the time you could devote to what is important in your life?

What effect did the worrying have on the people around you?

Did you do avoid anything or do in excess as a consequence (e.g. drink more, use drugs, binge eat, purge?)

Overall, how helpful was it to buy into your worrying?

Alternative Directions

What alternative direction could you find that are consistent with your goals and valued directions instead of worrying?

Is there a pattern to the situations that are typically linked to worrying that you could change? For example, can you do anything to prevent such situations (in the Activating Event)?

Cost-benefit analysis

To help say good riddance to worrying about your health it can be useful to do a 'cost-benefit' analysis on worry. In doing so you can consider the advantages and disadvantages of worrying about your health. When you do this exercise, consider the following:

- What are the advantages and disadvantages of worrying **in the short term**?
- What are the advantages and disadvantages of worrying **in the long term**?
- What are the advantages and disadvantages to **yourself** of worrying?
- What are the advantages and disadvantages **to other people** of worrying?

EXERCISE 5.2: COST-BENEFIT ANALYSIS: WORRY

Costs of worrying about my health	Benefits of worrying about my health

Next consider the pros and cons of reducing your worry about your health (to yourself and others).

EXERCISE 5.3: COST-BENEFIT ANALYSIS: REDUCING WORRY

Costs of reducing my worry about my health	Benefits of reducing my worry about my health

Motivations to worry

If you think it's reasonable to worry then it's very understandable that this worrying is something that you *do*. Furthermore, you are not in a strong position to develop the skills to overcome it. Having some *positive* beliefs about worry is extremely common, but the problem is sometimes compounded by the fact that people will then also worry that anxiety and worry *itself* might cause them harm. Being aware of how these thoughts might be steering you directly into health anxiety and considering whether these beliefs really are worth listening to will help you to overcome the problem.

Here are some examples of the positive beliefs and motivations that people with health anxiety have about worrying and being preoccupied about their health:

- *If I don't worry about my health I might miss something important.*
- *If I don't worry about my health I might regret not being careful enough if I become ill.*
- *Worrying means I don't have to think about the bad things that are happening in my life now.*
- *Thoughts about this illness must be on my mind for a reason, ignoring them is irresponsible.*
- *Ignoring thoughts about illness is tempting fate.*
- *If I don't worry I might neglect my health and become really unhealthy.*
- *Worrying will give me some hope of being mentally prepared for the worst.*

- *Because my particular feared illness is so awful it would be silly and irresponsible not to worry about it.*
- *Something like my health is so important that being certain everything is fine is the only way I could ever stop worrying.*
- *If a health professional has given me important information about my health I should remind myself of it regularly so that I don't forget it.*

EXERCISE 5.4: POSITIVE BELIEFS ABOUT WORRY

List your own positive beliefs about the process of worrying over your health. What are your most important beliefs that motivate you to worry about your health?

1 ....

....

2 ....

....

3 ....

....

4 ....

....

Negative beliefs about worry

It's very understandable for positive beliefs to promote worrying and increase your tendency to focus on your body and to carry out safety-seeking behaviors such as checking, seeking medical investigations and reassurance-seeking. Equally you may have a number of negative beliefs about worrying that make you anxious. Here are some examples of the *negative* beliefs and motivations that people with health anxiety give about worrying about their health:

- *If I worry too much then I might push my mind over the edge into a serious mental illness.*
- *If I worry then I won't be able to think straight and rationally.*
- *All this worry might be putting too much strain on my heart.*
- *I can't concentrate and I'll end up doing worse at work/school etc.*
- *I feel as if I'm losing my mind.*
- *I can't be the kind of friend/partner/parent etc. that I want to be because I can't cope with thinking about other things.*
- *I'm sure all this stress is making me more prone to illness/cancer.*
- *Because I'm so worried all the time people won't take me seriously.*

Again, it's easy to see how these thoughts may further compound the problem. The danger is that many people who suffer from heath anxiety try to deal with the negative aspects of worrying by simply trying harder to eliminate the uncertainties that they worry about. The downside is that this usually makes their worry worse, forming a vicious cycle.

EXERCISE 5.5: NEGATIVE BELIEFS ABOUT WORRY

What are your most important negative beliefs about the process of worrying? For example, 'Too much worrying will make me more stressed and make me ill.'

1 ______________________________

____

2 ______________________________

____

3 ______________________________

____

4 ______________________________

____

Now that you are more aware of the thoughts that influence your worrying you can begin to be less influenced by them and, we hope, ultimately come to detach from and ignore them.

Now reconsider your beliefs about worrying about your health. Consider each of your positive and negative beliefs you have listed above. The type of questions to ask yourself are:

- Does this belief about worrying help me to overcome my health anxiety?
- Does my belief help me to follow the directions in life that I want to follow? What alternative actions can I do?
- While I hold this belief about my worrying, do I become more preoccupied and act in ways that are unhelpful?
- Would I teach these attitudes about worrying about health to a child? If not why not?

In exercise 5.6 write down some alternative beliefs about worry that will help you develop a more appropriate level of concern about your health and enable you to free yourself from health anxiety. Here is an example:

EXERCISE 5.6: COMPARING BELIEFS ABOUT WORRY

Example.

Positive belief about worry: 'Worrying mentally prepares me for the worst'

Alternative belief about worry: 'In reality I can only deal with being diagnosed with a serious illness if and when it happens. Worry just makes me feel more anxious and interferes in my ability do things that are important now.'

Alternative actions: 'I can stop avoiding the situations I fear and just experience the intrusive thoughts and images when they are triggered without trying to solve them as current threats.'

Now consider your own beliefs:

Positive/negative belief: ______________________________

____

____

____

Alternative belief: ______________________________

____

____

____

Alternative actions: ______________________________

____

____

____

Now that you have a stronger commitment to overcome your tendency to worry we hope that you will now:

- try treating your problem 'as if' it is a worry problem;
- spot when you are engaging in the process of worrying excessively about your health;
- bring the focus of your mind back on to the outside world in the here and now;
- decide to deal with being mentally or physically ill or dying if/when it happens (we'll all eventually die somehow!);
- take a reasonable degree of care of your physical and mental health and get on with your what's important to you in your life in the meantime.

The following chapters in this book aim to help you learn to manage the re-focus your attention on to the outside world and less on your body/mind (Chapter 6) and to face situations you are currently avoiding so that you can reduce your fear and worry (Chapter 7).

6

Learning to re-train your attention

When people are anxious about something they tend to be especially vigilant, looking out for examples of whatever is worrying them. This is one of the helpful aspects of anxiety should we be in a genuinely threatening situation. For example, it's helpful to be watchful if we are at risk of being attacked by a wild animal. Our attention becomes very narrow in observing where the animal is and what its next move is going to be.

In the same way, if you have been pregnant, or have wanted to become pregnant, you may have noticed that suddenly the world seemed to be flooded with pregnant women and babies. How about if you or someone you know have just bought a new car? Have you found that you kept noticing the same make on the road? It's not that there are more babies being born, or more cars of the same model being bought; it's just that our attention is seeking out the subjects that interest us: it is *biased towards* noticing those subjects. What is on our minds will influence what we notice; it's just part of how the human brain works.

How about someone who is anxious about spiders or insects? Have you ever observed that they tend to see them where and when you hadn't noticed anything? When people are anxious about something they tend to be more *vigilant* for examples of it.

In health anxiety, this *attention bias* is one of the factors that keeps the condition going. For example:

- people with fears of being made ill through environmental toxins harm will tend to notice possible sources of chemicals and toxins;
- people who focus their attention internally on how they 'feel' will tend to magnify their anxiety and take it as evidence that there is a illness from which they need to solve;
- people who focus on their intrusive thoughts and ideas will find these tend to be magnified and appear more frequently;
- it's not unusual for people who are particularly preoccupied to even misread words that are close to the names of the illnesses they are afraid of; 'Chaucer St' becomes 'Cancer St';
- being vigilant for information about illness can lead to the sense that your feared illness is at near epidemic proportion.

Being self-focused means being on the outside looking back at yourself. It means being very aware of your thoughts, feelings, mental images, and body sensations. Being focused on life means being on the inside and looking out at the world around you and at what you can touch, taste, feel, see, hear or smell. People with health anxiety are frequently self-focused and constantly monitoring their body or mind for possible symptoms of their feared illness.

Self-focused attention can also have a big effect on your overall mood. Spending a lot of time going over problems in your thoughts serves only to heighten stress on your mind and body. Refocusing your attention onto the outside world gives your brain a rest and allows you to take in what the world has to offer. Overcoming health anxiety will mean broadening your attention to take everything in, not just focusing on your body or mind, and refocusing your attention away from your inner world.

EXERCISE 6.1: WHAT DO YOU FOCUS ON?

Take a moment to consider the past day or past week, and try to identify what you tend to notice more of than the average person in the street. Do you monitor your thoughts, images or body sensations or part of your body? Do you look out for threats and dangers?

I'm over-aware of ______________________

1 ______________________

2 ______________________

3 ______________________

Figure 6.1 Vicious cycle of attention bias

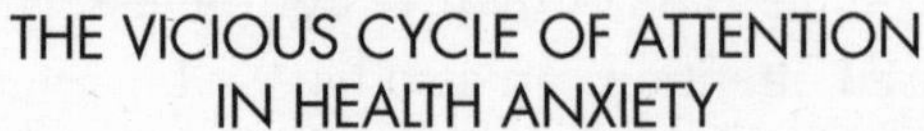

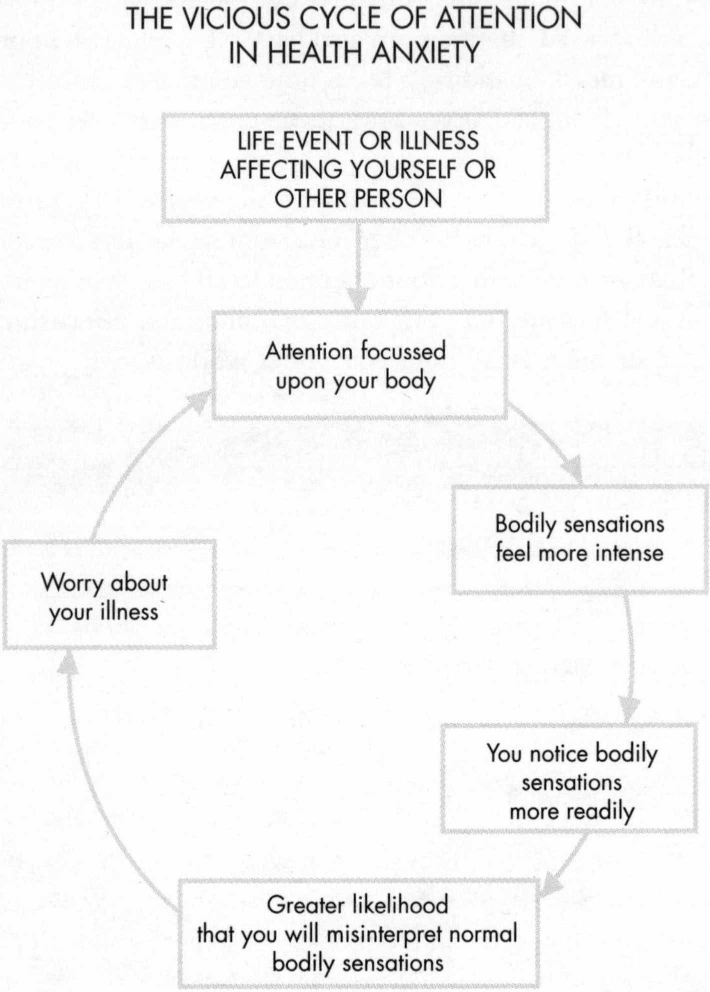
THE VICIOUS CYCLE OF ATTENTION
IN HEALTH ANXIETY
LIFE EVENT OR ILLNESS
AFFECTING YOURSELF OR
OTHER PERSON
Attention focussed
upon your body
Bodily sensations
feel more intense
You notice bodily
sensations
more readily
Greater likelihood
that you will misinterpret normal
bodily sensations
Worry about
your illness

Biased attention fuels biased conclusions

For example, if you constantly monitor the world and yourself for illness, you will see the world as a potentially dangerous place and yourself as vulnerable. If you are very tuned in to your body, its lumps, bumps, physical sensations, and mental sensations you are far more likely to jump to a conclusion that there's something wrong if you notice a minor change. This means you might experience distressing anxiety about a physical experience that the average person on the street might not have even noticed. We hope that this understanding helps you to see the benefit of learning to re-direct and become more flexible in where you focus your attention rather than it being frequently hijacked by your health anxiety. The remainder of this chapter focuses upon identifying the thoughts and beliefs that drive you to over-focus your attention on your body and health, and how to re-train your attention back on to the outside world.

Understanding your motivation for being overly self-focused

If you are overly self-focused, and you are having difficulty in switching your attention externally, it may be helpful to explore a) the situations in which you tend to be self-focused; b) the benefits you think you get from being self-focused; and c) the motivation for being self-focused. The exercise below will help you to understand what is causing you to become overly self-focused.

EXERCISE 6.2: QUESTIONING YOUR MOTIVATION

What is your motivation for being self-focused?

Do you sometimes think that being self-focused could help you? Do you feel that it might prepare you for illness or something bad happening? Use the space below to write down your own motivations – try using assumptions, such as, 'If I am self-focused I can prevent myself from missing something important about my health.'

While doing this exercise, ask yourself the following questions:

- Does this assumption about being self-focused help me achieve my goals and valued directions in life?
- Would I recommend that others bias their attention in this way?
- What doubts do I have about being externally focused and concentrating on my tasks or what I see, hear and smell?
- Is the cost of being self-focused too high?

Now decide whether holding such assumptions about being self-focused is really helpful and whether you could try an alternative, in other words try being externally focused. Write down below what you plan to focus on in your external environment.

EXERCISE 6.3: WHAT DO YOU PLAN TO FOCUS UPON THE EXTERNAL WORLD?

Monitoring your self-focused attention

In any given situation, especially when you are feeling especially anxious or withdrawn, you can estimate the percentage of your attention that is focused on:

a) yourself (e.g. monitoring how you appear to others or how you feel)
b) your tasks (e.g. listening or talking to someone or writing)
c) your environment (e.g. the hum of traffic in the background).

The three must add up to 100 per cent, and the ratio is likely to vary in different situations. When you are very self-focused, about 80 per cent of your attention might be on yourself, about 10 per cent on the task you are involved in, and 10 per cent on your environment. Someone *without* health anxiety might normally focus about 10 per cent on him- or herself, 80 per cent on the task, and 10 per cent on the environment. This is an important observation because it means you can train yourself to be more focused on tasks and the environment and less on yourself.

Rating your attention percentages

How self-focused are you? Over the next few days, use Exercise 6.4 to make a note of different situations (e.g. reading about someone dying form cancer, talking to someone of the opposite sex of the same age, reading, etc) and then rate the approximate percentage of your attention that is on:

a) yourself (0–100 per cent)
b) your task (0–100 per cent)
c) your environment (0–100 per cent)
(Remember the three above must add up to 100 per cent)
d) degree of distress (0–100 per cent).

Try to compare the same situation with a different percentage of attention on yourself. For example, compare talking to someone you know well:

a) Being very self-focused (for example 80 per cent of attention on a physical or mental sensation)

b) Concentrating on what you are saying and really listening to your friend (for example, 80 per cent attention on the task)

How does your degree of distress compare in a) and b)?

What effect does your change in attention focus have on your friend? Does he or she find you warmer and friendlier?

Adjusting your attention

We hope we have convinced you that it can be helpful to reduce your self-focused attention. When this is difficult, you can use specific exercises that have been proven to help people focus their attention better on the outside world. Think of these exercises as helping you to build the psychological muscle that places your attention on the world around you, rather than on yourself.

Situational refocusing

This technique involves immediately refocusing your mind on the task you're involved in or on the environment around you whenever you notice that you are becoming self-focused (say, above 50 per cent of attention focused on yourself). Practise being absorbed in a particular task (e.g. having a conversation) and when you notice your attention is drawn towards yourself, deliberately refocus your attention away from yourself on to something else around you. Similarly, if you tend to focus all the time on how you feel, refocus attention outside yourself on some practical task in hand

EXERCISE 6.4: MONITORING SELF-FOCUSED ATTENTION CHART

Date	Situation	% attention on self	% attention on task	% attention environment	Total (100%)	Distress (0–100%)

or on the environment around you. Every time you notice your mind's endless chatter and focus on how you feel, refocus your attention back on to the task or your environment. As a guide, try to aim for self-focused attention in most contexts to be reduced to 30 per cent or less.

If you are alone and have no specific task to do, you will need to refocus on your environment and make yourself more aware of:

- the various objects, colours, people, patterns and shapes that you can see around you (e.g. fabrics, decor, cars on the street, trees, litter)
- the sounds that you can hear (e.g. the hum of a heater, the sound off traffic, a clock ticking)
- what you can smell (e.g. scent of flowers, traffic fumes, fresh air, fabric softener)
- what you can taste (e.g. in the case of food or drink)
- the physical sensations you can feel from the environment (e.g. whether hot or cold, whether there is a breeze, the hardness of the ground beneath your feet).

Re-training your attention

This technique is called 'attentional training' and it was devised by the psychologist Adrian Wells from Manchester University. It will help you reduce self-focused attention in the long term and increase your flexibility at switching attention.

This technique has been shown to be of some benefit in health anxiety for reducing self-focused attention in the long term. It is a form of mental training, like going to a psychological gym and getting your attention muscles in shape. It is also something you can practise at home, rather like practising a musical instrument in your room in readiness for playing with an orchestra.

The following exercise should be practised when you are alone and not distracted. In other words, this is not a technique you should use to distract yourself when you feel upset or are brooding – it needs to be practised when you are alone, alert and not especially distressed. In the long term the training can help you to interrupt the cycle of being self-focused so that you eventually become more naturally aware of your external environment. The technique may seem difficult at first but it is worth persevering with and doing in small steps.

Monitoring how self-focused you are

You can monitor how self-focused you are at any given moment on a scale of between -3 and +3, where -3 represents being entirely focused on your own thoughts and feelings or the impression you have of yourself, and +3 means being entirely externally focused on a task (e.g. listening to someone) or the environment (e.g. what you can see or hear). A zero would indicate that your attention is divided equally between being self-focused and externally focused. Being overly self-focused is a rating of -2 or -3.

Getting ready: Identify sounds and locations

The exercise involves collecting together three or more sounds, and some locations (which may or may not have consistent sound) to 'tune-in' to. You should aim for about nine sounds/locations, and label each one as sound/location 1, sound/location 2, and so on.

Examples of sounds are:

- the hum of a computer
- a tap dripping
- a radio at a low volume
- a hi-fi
- a vacuum cleaner in a room next door
- the noise of traffic
- a ticking clock.

Examples of locations are:

- outside, near by
- outside in the far distance
- a location (e.g. a room or a building) to the left
- a location (e.g. a room or a building) to the right
- a room below or above.

EXERCISE 6.5: SOUNDS AND LOCATIONS

Write down your sounds and locations:

1 ____________________

2 ____________________

3 ____________________

4 ____________________

5 ____________________

6 ____________________

7 ____________________

8 ____________________

9 ____________________

Phase 1: Five minutes' slowly switching between sounds/locations

Sit down in a comfortable chair, relax and focus your gaze on a spot on the wall. You should keep your eyes open throughout. You may experience distracting thoughts, feelings or images that just pop into your mind during the exercise. This doesn't matter – allow them to happen. The aim is to practise focusing your attention in a particular way. Focus your attention on each of the sounds in the sequence in a sustained manner. Pay close attention to sound number one, telling yourself that no other sound matters. Ignore all the other sounds around you. Now focus on the sound number two. Focus only on that sound, again telling yourself that no other sound matters. If your attention begins to stray or is captured by any other sound, refocus all your attention on sound number two. Give all your attention to that sound. Focus on that sound, monitor it closely and filter out all the competing sounds, for they are not significant. Go through all the sounds/locations in sequence until you have reached sound number nine.

Phase 2: Five minutes' rapid switching

Now move on to the second phase. You have identified and focused on all the sounds. In this next stage we want you to rapidly shift attention from one sound to another in a random order. For example, you could pass from sound number six to number four to three to nine to one, and so on. As before, focus all your attention on one sound before switching your attention to a different sound.

Phase 3: Two minutes' holding all sounds/locations in your attention together

Then move on to the third phase. Expand all your attention, make it as broad and deep as possible and try to absorb all the sounds simultaneously. Mentally count all the sounds you can hear at the same time.

Practising the exercise

The exercise needs to be practised twice a day (or a minimum of once a day) for 12–15 minutes. If possible, try to introduce new sounds on each occasion so you don't get used to them. We appreciate that this is difficult. Keep a record of your attention training on the chart below. Like physical training, the exercise needs to be practised repeatedly or your attention muscles won't get bigger. Keep a note on a calendar or a diary using a tick to record when you did your practice. This will help you keep track of whether you are keeping up your mental fitness program!

EXERCISE 6.6 RECORD OF ATTENTION TRAINING

Rating scale

−3: entirely focused on your own thoughts and feelings or the impression you have of yourself
0: attention divided equally between being self-focused and externally focused
+3: entirely externally focused on a task (e.g. listening to someone) or the environment (e.g. what you can see or hear)

Date	How self-focused I have been generally today (−3 to +3)	How long the training lasted	Number of sounds I used	Any other comments

7

Reducing anxiety by facing your fears

Most people know that a key way to reduce your fear is to face it. You may have heard of 'facing your fears' as the main treatment for phobias, such as fear of spiders, birds or snakes. In the case of health anxiety the 'fear' is not just of a situation or activity, but also of the thoughts, images, doubts, and sensations that it triggers. Psychologists call the therapeutic use of facing your fears *exposure*. When it is combined with resisting rituals such as checking and reassurance-seeking it is called *exposure and response-prevention*. This process can be viewed as a 'behavioral experiments' to test out a prediction that you making about what you experience. One of your predictions might be how severe the distress is going to be, or how long it might go on for at the end of exposure. Or it may be helpful to test whether the result of the exposure bests fits 'Theory A' or 'Theory B' (see Chapter 2).

Theory A (the one that you are following) is that you have a medial condition Theory B is that you have a problem with being excessively worried by your health. This predicts that by following Theory A you are increasing your worry and distress about your health. When you act as if Theory

B is right, then your worry and distress about your health will decrease.

Another way of looking at health anxiety is to understand it as a problem of having become intolerant of particular doubts about your health. Thus you can view facing your fears and deliberately provoking those doubts as a way of giving yourself an opportunity to practice becoming more tolerant of uncertainty.

Dropping safety behaviours

Exposure also needs to be done without using any safety-seeking behaviors. A safety-seeking behavior is an action taken within a feared situation in order to prevent harm. The action is intended to prevent a catastrophe and/or reduce harm. Safety-seeking behaviors in health anxiety include many different ways of escaping and trying to cope – for example, carefully monitoring your heart rate for fear of having a stroke; reassuring yourself or trying to keep control of your thoughts to prevent yourself from becoming schizophrenic. However, safety behaviors can have a number of unintended consequences. They may prevent you from finding out that what you are predicting is not true. They also tend to make you more aware of your physical sensations, more preoccupied with your health and more distressed, as you also have to monitor whether your safety behavior is working.

Frequency recording for checking

If this is a problem for you then the first step is to see how often you are checking your body or attempting to reassure yourself by reviewing information. You can do this using a record sheet like the one below. Some people check 30, 50 or hundreds of times a day. If this is the case with you, it's best to use a tally counter and to carry over the total to the chart. This method will tell you exactly how often you are checking and will give you a baseline so that you can tell in future whether or not your checking is decreasing over time.

Keeping a record will also make you more aware of when you are checking so that you can resist it in future. Add a tick or a click on your tally counter whenever you do any of these checking activities.

This is an example of a record sheet:

SAMPLE FREQUENCY OF CHECKING

	Mon	Tues	Wed	Thurs	Fri	Sat	Sun
Seeking reassurance from my wife		✓			✓✓✓	✓✓✓	✓
Checking my stools	✓✓	✓	✓		✓✓		✓✓
Reassuring myself in my mind	✓	✓	✓	✓	✓	✓	✓
Searching on the Internet		✓	✓	✓	✓✓✓	✓✓✓ ✓✓✓	✓✓
Pressing my stomach					✓✓✓ ✓✓✓ ✓	✓✓✓ ✓✓✓ ✓	✓✓✓

EXERCISE 7.1: FREQUENCY OF CHECKING OR REASSURANCE

Date ______________

	Mon	Tues	Wed	Thurs	Fri	Sat	Sun

Throw out any health paraphernalia

If you have any text books, test-kits, monitors, special alternative remedies aimed at warding off illness that you know, in your heart of hearts, that you would not possess if you were not excessively worried about your health. If you have health anxiety you need to be less focussed about health problems at the moment than the average person, not less. So if in doubt – chuck it out!

Anxiety is nothing to be afraid of

It's quite common in health anxiety to fear that too much anxiety can be harmful. It's true that exposure is often done in a graded manner, with a series of steps (called a 'hierarchy'), so that you face your less intimidating fears first and confront the most difficult last. But grading your exposure is just a means to an end, and the sooner you can reach the top of your exposure hierarchy the better. Remember that anxiety, though uncomfortable, will not damage you. If you approach your fears too gradually, you'll only reinforce the idea that anxiety is potentially harmful.

Make sure your exposure is long enough

With any exposure program, it really is important to stick with the session until your anxiety has reduced by at least half, otherwise you may end up reinforcing the idea that anxiety is harmful. On average, exposure might take up to an hour, but sometimes it doesn't take that long. If the anxiety is persisting for longer than this, then you may be performing a subtle safety behavior or not fully engaging in the exposure. Think really carefully about whether you are doing anything to temporarily reduce or control your fear within the situation. If you think that something you are doing might just be a way of staving off your fear, try your exposure without it.

Figure 7.1 opposite demonstrates what happens when your fear is triggered and when you experience fear *without* a safety behavior. The anxiety gradually fades over time and the urge to use your safety behavior will also fade. When you repeat the exposure (preferably as soon after the first exposure as possible), the anxiety will decrease further, and so on each time you do the exposure.

One way of remembering what exposure and response prevention means is the 'FEAR' acronym:

Face
Everything
And
Recover.

Here are some examples of ways to face your fears of ill health and death:

- Writing out and repeatedly reading over a description of your feared event, such as sitting in the doctors office being told that you are seriously ill and have only a few months to live. Write this

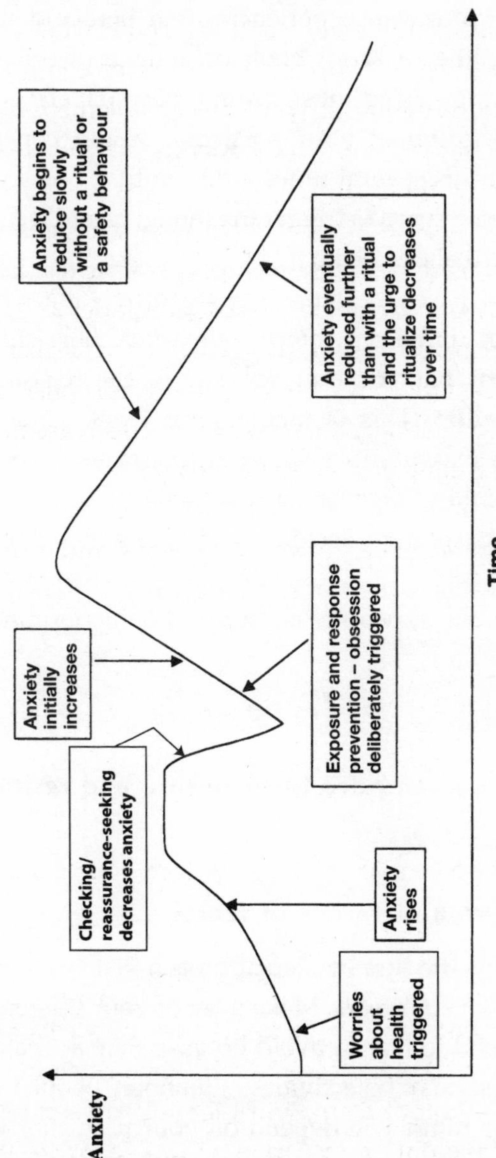

Figure 7.1 Effect of exposure and response prevention on anxiety within a session

out as if your were experiencing it in 'here-and now'.

- Put together a scrap book or collage of anxiety-provoking headlines from newspapers and magazines about your particular health concern. Look at this several times a day until it bores you.
- Visit a graveyard to trigger the thoughts and feelings you have about death.
- Cut and paste the more anxiety provoking words you can find from internet websites. It is crucial however that you edit out any of the reassuring information. This is facing your fears – not yet another reassurance session. If reassurance worked you wouldn't be reading this book!
- Visit a hospital or accident and emergency department.
- Read books of peoples accounts of being terminally ill.

The eleven golden rules for exposure and response prevention

1 Write down a hierarchy of fears

A 'hierarchy' is the step-by-step approach that you carry out in order to face your fears. Make a list of your triggers – the things you tend to fear or avoid because they activate your worries. These may be activities, situations, people, words or ideas – the range will depend on your particular worry.

The nature of an exposure task will depend upon your

problem and whether you are someone who is avoiding lots of situations or activities (where it's easier to come up with suitable exposure) or if you are a person who has lots of safety-seeking behaviors (such as checking). You may also be avoiding images or thoughts about developing an illness or dying. These too can be added to the hierarchy.

You can measure the amount of distress caused by each trigger using a rating scale of 'SUDs'. SUDs stands for Standard Units of Distress, in which 0 is 'no distress at all' and 100 is 'the most distress' you can imagine. In the second column of the table, you can give each trigger a rating according to how much distress you would expect to feel if you experienced that trigger and didn't perform a safety behavior.

Here is a sample hierarchy table:

PAUL'S HIERARCHY OF EXPOSURE TO FEARED TRIGGERS

Trigger (object, place, person, situation, thought, image)	Estimated distress (0–100)
Visit an oncology ward	90
Write out and repeatedly read 'story' of doctor delivering the bad news that I've got bowel cancer, and that I would have survived had I caught it earlier	90
Read stories of people who have died of cancer	80
Read stories of people developing cancer after they had been reassured by their doctor that things are OK	80
Look at images of cancerous tumours	70
Read John Diamond's book 'C' about his experience of cancer	70

Now devise your own exposure hierarchy.

EXERCISE 7.2: HIERARCHY OF EXPOSURE TO FEARED TRIGGERS

Trigger (object, place, person, situation, thought, image)	Estimated distress (0–100)

2 Face your fear – 'just do it'

Decide which targets you will take from your hierarchy and deliberately face your fear. Choose targets that are challenging but not overwhelming. However, don't spend too much time on the easier targets, if they are not sufficiently challenging. You may need to ask a friend to come up with suitable tasks that are more anxiety-provoking. Always ensure that your exposure is challenging and potent enough.

3 Make predictions that can be tested

One of your predictions might be how severe the distress is going to be, or how long it might go on for at the end of exposure. Or it may be helpful to test whether the result of the exposure best fits 'Theory A' or 'Theory B'.

Theory A (the one that you are following) is that you have an physical illness. Theory B is that you have a problem with being excessively worried by your health. This predicts that by following Theory A you are increasing your worry, preoccupation and distress about your health. When you act as if Theory B is right, then your preoccupation and distress about your health will decrease.

Keep a record of your predictions and whether they occurred or not on your record sheet on pages 146–7.

4 Make exposure long enough

Face your fear long enough for your anxiety to subside of its own accord, ideally by at least half. Anxiety will decrease only when you give it a long enough time and learn that bad things won't happen when you face your fears.

5 Make exposure frequent enough

Repeat the exposure as often as possible – several times a day – until the anxiety has subsided between the sessions. Always think about how you can incorporate exposure into your everyday life so that it makes it easier to carry it out on a daily basis.

6 Make exposure continuous

Ensure exposure is done with a constant stimulus (trigger), rather than escaping or using a safety behavior.

7 Avoid anxiety-reducing strategies

Do the exposure without using distraction, drugs, alcohol, or a safety-seeking behavior such as saying a phrase to yourself or obtaining reassurance.

8 If you do a safety-seeking behavior, then re-expose yourself

If you can't resist doing a safety behavior (such as checking or reassurance-seeking), you must redo the exposure so that you always finish with your anxiety having reduced of its own accord.

9 Let intrusive thoughts and images pass

'Notice' or 'be aware' of any unpleasant images that might occur during the exposure without engaging with them or trying to push them away. Just allow yourself to experience these thoughts and images as passing events in your mind.

EXERCISE 7.3: RECORD OF EXPERIMENTS FOR ________ (DATE)

1 Task that I planned (e.g. when, where, how, and with whom. Include a description of how I will act without safety-seeking behaviors)	2 How distressing I am predicting task will be at the peak (0–100%)	3 How long I am predicting that the distress will take to halve (minutes or hours)	4 What I am predicting will happen or whether the result will best fit Theory A or Theory B and how strongly I believe it (0–100%)

5 What I actually did during the task (including using any safety-seeking behaviors and degree of self-focused attention)	6 How distressing the task was at the peak (0–100%)	7 How long it actually took for the distress to halve (minutes or hours)	8 What actually happened? Does this differ from what I predicted in column 4? Do the results best fit my theory that I have a problem with my health or the alternative – that the problem is being excessively worried about my health?

10 Monitor your progress

Always monitor your exposure so you can learn from it and see your progress. Re-rate your distress at the end of exposure and see whether you over-estimated the degree of distress that would occur or how long it would last for.

11 Maintain motivation

Keep focussing on why you are doing all this hard work. In Chapter 3 you completed a 'valued directions' questionnaire. The reason why you are experiencing some distress now is so you can do the things in life that are important to you.

Obstacles

The problem with 'normal' – treatment first, normal later

You might be concerned at some of the suggestions that a therapist or we might make for exposure at the top of your hierarchy but they are a means towards an end. As soon as you have overcome your health anxiety, you can bin them. People sometimes complain that what they are being encouraged to do during exposure is 'abnormal' and therefore unreasonable.

If you think about it, many treatments for human ailments involve doing the unusual. Consider how 'abnormal' it is to swallow toxic chemicals every day, but chemotherapy treatment for cancer involves exactly that. Likewise, it's not exactly normal to wrap a leg in plaster, but if you have a broken leg, it's very helpful! We accept these 'abnormal' activities as part of 'normal' treatment for physical problems.

So remember, if you are reading this book as part of your plan to overcome your health anxiety, your exposure can be enhanced by testing out the predictions that you are making. However, this needs to be frequent enough, long enough, and 'potent' enough and without safety-seeking behaviors to reduce your feeling of threat. Would you expect a medication to be effective if you took less than the recommended dose and took it less often than prescribed?

8

Getting the most from your doctor

In an attempt to put your mind at rest you may be seeking frequent reassurance from your family doctor or going direct to various specialists. Doctors generally want to help you and will order a new test in the hope that it will reassure you and exclude anything serious.

Quite often, in listening to a patient's history a doctor begins to form a diagnosis even before any examination. The processes of examining you and receiving a positive test result just confirms what the doctor already knew or gives the doctor the location of the problem. If an examination or a test is found to be negative then it will reassure a patient and that is the end of the matter. However, getting reassurance from a doctor or receiving a negative test result does not usually help someone with health anxiety in the long term. This is because reassurance only works in the short term. It doesn't take long before a doubt pops into your mind about what the doctor might have missed.

Even before you get the results, you may be thinking that having a test must mean that the doctor thinks there is something wrong with you. As we have already discussed, doctors normally operate like this but they have a different motivation from someone with health anxiety – they are examining you or ordering a test to reassure you. Or they may give you an unnecessary medication to reduce your symptoms. In other words, they are buying into your anxiety because they don't want to see you suffer. The same sequence of events can take place if you see an alternative practitioner. He or she may provide a credible explanation (e.g. you have an allergy or your meridians are wrong) and then prescribe a remedy. Alternative practitioners are often popular because they have more time than your family doctor to listen you. They may be very compassionate and make you feel understood.

The results of an examination or a test or a new remedy may be helpful initially. Sometimes the symptom goes away, usually because body sensations are self-limiting and go away by themselves. But then the doubts return. Sometimes the worry moves on to a different area of the body, with a new symptom. Sometimes the doubts about the original test persist. In general the more times you check something, the more that checking increases your doubt. Even if a test is negative the doubt might be 'What if it's something else the doctor has missed?', 'What if the laboratory made a mistake?', 'What if the test doesn't pick up what I've got?'.

Sometimes posting message on a bulletin board can make things worse because other well-meaning individuals will suggest tests that you need and what to say to your doctor. There are number of possible disadvantages and unintended consequences from frequently seeking reassurance from your doctors.

a) The more tests you have, the more likely you are to have a false positive. This is a result that suggests something positive but which is a mistake. This usually leads to more false leads and unnecessary tests to exclude the positive result. This in turn increases your doubts and worries.
b) Some doctors use medical terms that sound impressive but are fairly meaningless or descriptions of a normal variation in everyone. For example, androgenic alopecia simply means normal male pattern baldness. Premature atrial contractions of the heart are usually perfectly normal or related to caffeine or exercise. Using medical terminology feeds your doubts by making a condition sound pathological when it it's quite normal variation.
c) Some tests are painful or have a risk of causing an illness. We have seen people with chest pain caused by anxiety have an X-ray that involves catheterization of the cardiac vessels. This is an important investigation if you have heart disease since it tells a surgeon exactly where to operate – however, there is a small risk it could cause a heart attack. This is a risk worth taking if it is to save your life in an operation, but it is not an investigation to reassure someone they do not have heart disease.
d) Most doctors are caring and do not want you to suffer. If you seeking help privately, less scrupulous doctors might cotton on to your fears and will provide you with as much reassurance and tests as you want, partly for a financial motive. Thus

in some countries, like the United States, there are many more investigations than in the United Kingdom, but US citizens are not healthier. Even in a public service, some doctors will order as many tests as you want in a genuine desire to reassure you. Doctors may also be acting defensively and be driven more by a fear of litigation and a concern not to miss anything important. In summary, some doctors may be more anxious and cannot tolerate uncertainty – so they order more tests so they can feel less anxious even if other doctors might think such tests to be unnecessary.

e) Over time a doctor might develop a jaundiced view of your worries and privately label you as a hypochondriac. They might not listen to you seriously when you really do have a problem. We don't think this happens very often but it's very understandable if you have been complaining of various symptoms for many years, none of which has been serious.

How to get the most from your doctor

1 It is important to maintain a good relationship with your family doctor. Use one doctor whom you trust and who understands your history of health anxiety – don't doctor shop. This includes seeking reassurance from friends who are doctors or alternative health practitioners.
2 Ask your doctor to treat you like any other patient. If the doctor is concerned about a symptom and

wants to exclude something serious then he will order a test. He or she should not order a test with the aim of reassuring you – because this does not help your mental health. Nearly all diagnoses can be made from examining your history. Sometimes a physical examination or test may add some extra information or confirm a doctor's diagnosis, but it rarely picks up anything new. Equally, it is important not to refer to yet another medical specialist – it's more important to refer you to a cognitive behavior therapist who can follow a protocol for treating health anxiety.

3 Only you can experience your pain or symptom. No one else can know what you feel. You can't 'imagine' your pain and if a doctor tells you that you are just imagining things, then it's probably better to find one who can better understand health anxiety. It's true that some of the ways you cope may be aggravating your symptoms, for example repeatedly pressing on a body part to check for lumps might make you sore and swollen.

4 Try to choose a doctor who can you understand your distress but gives you relevant information about the cause of your symptoms (e.g. 'the chest pain that you experience is caused by tension from the muscles in your chest wall') and can then demonstrate to you how the symptoms come about. What is less helpful is bland reassurance that you have not got what you fear you've got or repetition of the same information. So it's important to try to

train your doctor to explain to you what your symptoms are, not what they are not.

5 When you have persistent symptoms, it may be difficult for you and your doctor to know when to stop having investigations. You may want to stop having tests when you feel 'comfortable' or it feels 'right'. In other words, not only do you want the test result to be negative but you also want them to change the way you feel. Unfortunately, negative test results don't always lead you to feel comfortable and can be an unhelpful way of trying to change the way you feel.

It is acceptable medical practice to wait and see what happens (i.e. to ask you to come back in three months' time) for many unexplained or persistent symptoms when the history does not suggest anything serious. If you have had a relevant investigation, then a new test is very unlikely to reveal anything new. Some people find that continuing appointments with their doctor and the provision of various remedies (such as bandages, lotions, vitamins, heat pads, massage) helps to provide tangible evidence of their doctor's understanding and acknowledgement of their suffering.) In general we think it is better to focus your energy on doing things in life despite your symptoms and not to medicalize your symptoms – and to really commit yourself to treating them as a health anxiety problem.

One good option is to sign up to a psychological therapy for three months and if, after that period, your symptoms persist, you can always go back to your doctor and ask him or her to think again and obtain another opinion. When we say commit yourself, this will mean consistently dropping all your avoidance and checking behaviors and acting as if you have problem of health anxiety (even if you aren't 100 per cent convinced). It will mean not seeking reassurance for your symptom or researching it more on the Internet. It means not mentally planning your next investigation or doctor to visit. It also means giving up no longer reassuring yourself or trying to solve your mental health problem as a physical problem.

6 If you have a medical problem like diabetes it will be more difficult for the doctor to sort out what should be investigated and what may be related to your health anxiety. Again, your doctor should treat you like any other patient with the same medical problem and only investigate a symptom if he or she wants to and not because you want to be reassured.

9

Overcoming health anxiety in action

Adrian's fear of having a heart attack

Adrian was aged forty-five. Most of his life he had been a worrier, but this had not been a major problem. He had become increasingly worried about his heart after he felt that is was missing beats. He'd had several consultations with his doctor, who had reassured him that there was no evidence of a heart problem. Adrian checked his pulse and blood pressure daily. To try to put his mind at rest his doctor sent him to see a specialist heart doctor. Adrian's reaction to this referral was that he thought 'My doctor must be more concerned than he's saying, otherwise he wouldn't have sent me for a test.' This meant that his anxiety became much worse the following week, and eventually he paid to see a private heart specialist, who carried out some 24-hour ECG testing and reported back that he could lose a bit of weight but his test results were within normal limits.

Feeling satisfied after his appointment, it occurred to Adrian that he might have not given the cardiologist all of the information he needed. What if he did not have a big enough missed beat on the day of the test? He spent hours trying to think of better ways of describing his symptoms, becoming ever more preoccupied and distressed. He would switch between this and trying to reassure himself by telling himself to be more rational and pull himself together. This led to more doubts and checking on the Internet. He became an expert on his own heart rhythm and became convinced that his heart was fragile and more prone than average to problems.

Key aspects of Adrian's recovery

Adrian was initially very resistant to the notion that he had health anxiety, believing he was being fobbed off by his doctor whom he felt 'doesn't know what else to do with me'. Developing two alternative theories about the nature of his problem was then a crucial first step: Theory A ran 'I've got a heart problem that no one can pin-point', and Theory B ran 'I'm overly preoccupied and anxious and worry that I've got a heart problem.' He then began to consider the possibility that his very consciousness about his heart could be making him more prone to misinterpret normal changes in rhythm as signs of a problem. He then resisted his urges to check his pulse and blood pressure or to seek out more information on the Internet. He demonstrated to himself that if he really concentrated on different body parts, such as his fingertips, he would notice sensations he would otherwise be unaware of. Adrian then decided to try out treating his problem 'as if' it was an

Adrian's avoidance and safety behaviors

Figure 9.1 Vicious flower: Adrian's example

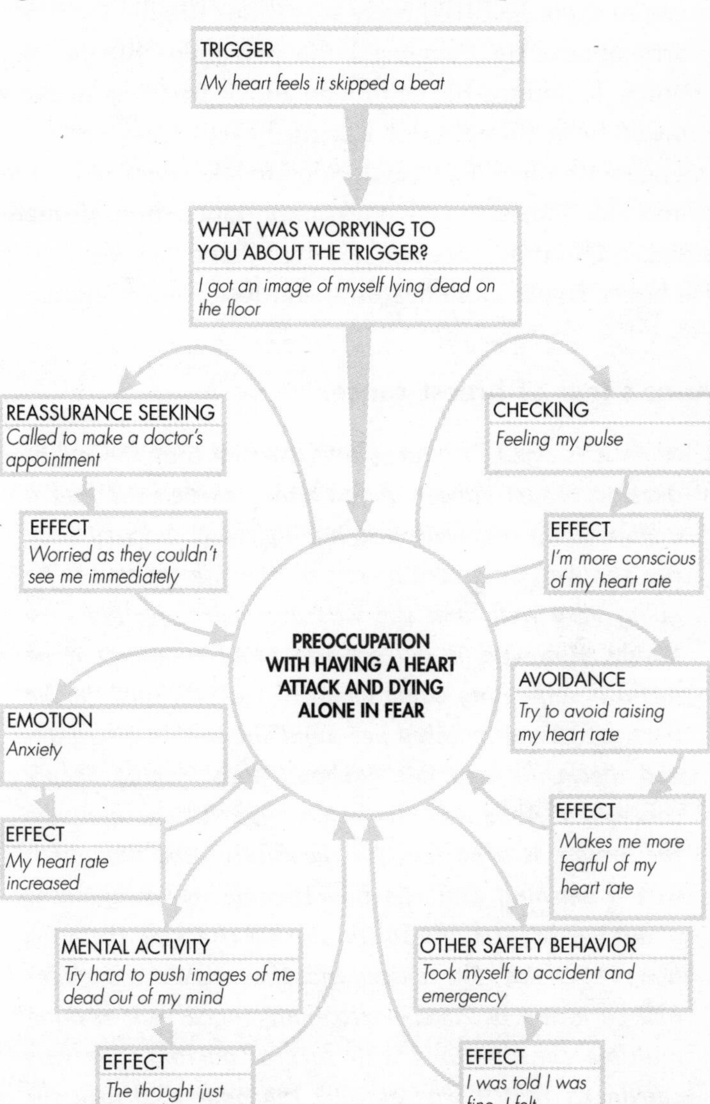

attention, preoccupation and anxiety problem. He educated himself on common symptoms of anxiety, noticing that many of them involved body sensations that he tended to worry about, He then used the principles of attention training to reduce his self-focus and learned to distance himself from thoughts of having heart disease and not engage with them. He also decided to take stock of his life, re-focusing himself on what was important to him. He made a will and his preoccupation with his heart slowly decreased. He began to eat more healthily and lose some weight.

Anne's fear of breast cancer

Anne was aged fifty-three and worried that she might develop breast cancer. A few years earlier she had a benign lump removed, and hadn't really worried until her son won an award at school. Her life seemed to be going very well, and she was in general feeling very happy. However, it crossed her mind 'wouldn't it be awful if something came along to spoil all this'. In the next image that entered her mind she was in a hospital bed, her child and her husband both looking deeply concerned. Anne was somewhat superstitious and saw the image as a portent for the future. She thought it was a warning that she had become too complacent about her breasts and so she started checking them for lumps each day. She noticed that they were more tender and sore and became increasingly concerned, seeking multiple consultations with several doctors. She was convinced that it was entirely reasonable to look for certainty about something as important as her health. She believed that none of the doctors she saw took a detailed enough interest in her concerns, thus becoming increasingly worried that something might have been missed.

Key aspects of Anne's recovery

Anne recorded the frequency of her checking on a tally counter and began to cut it down. Because her breasts were sore and bruised from her vigorous checking she readily decided this should be an early target (see Chapter 3). She also used a 'responsibility pie chart' on keeping her family happy, to help herself see that the responsibility did not fall wholly on her shoulders and that it would not be the absolute end of the world if she did become ill again. She used a cost-benefit analysis chart (see Chapter 5) and reduced her checking to once a month. She deliberately brought on the image of her dying and in her mind made it in into a tragic comedy – that she was to die a slow lingering death from breast cancer and before she died both her children and husband would die in a car accident on their way to visit her. She reproduced the original image in a painting of herself dying. Anne made arrangements for happy family occasions, focusing upon feeling gratitude for her happy life, and allowing any thoughts about it being spoiled to pass through her mind without engaging with them.

Anne's avoidance and safety behaviors

Figure 9.2 Vicious flower: Anne's example

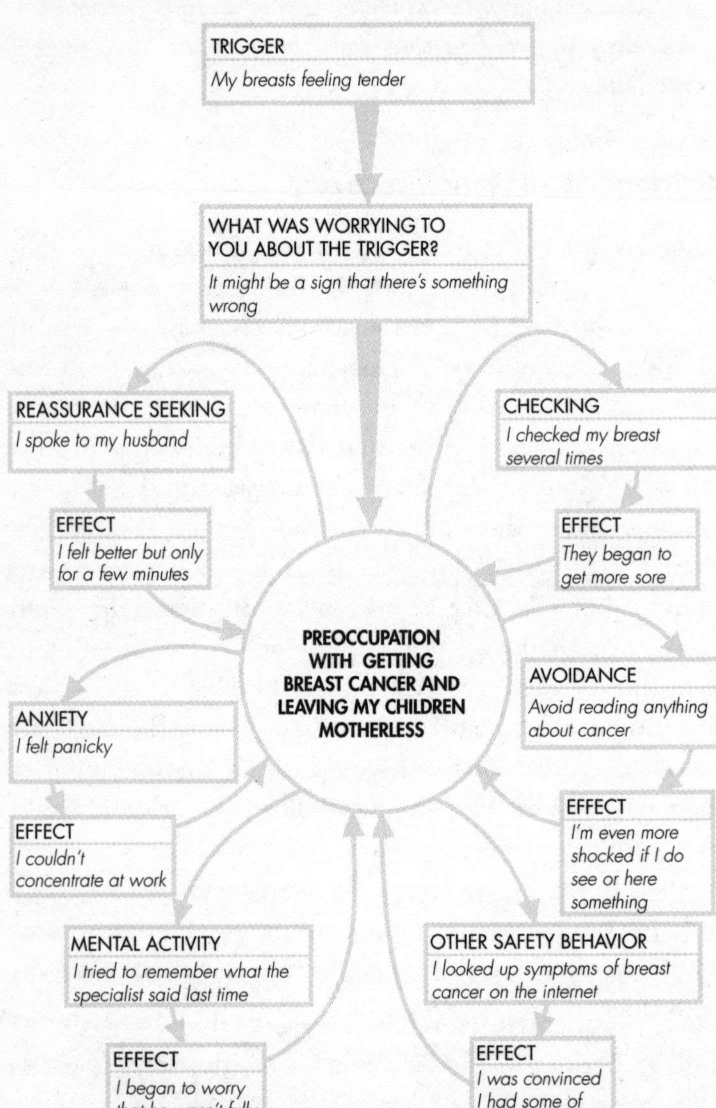

Steven's fear of going mad

Steven was preoccupied by a fear that he would go mad. He had an unhappy childhood since his father was alcoholic and the family had lived in fear of his rages. Steven was terrified that he would lose control of his mind, develop schizophrenia, fail to respond to treatment, end up in a locked psychiatric ward, lose his job, wife, house and children. He had a mental image of looking through the narrow window of a hospital ward and watching his wife and children visit. They looked sad since they were coming to terms with the fact that Steven was irretrievably lost to mental illness. He therefore checked his thoughts for any sign of madness or signs of unreality. One of his main anxiety symptoms was of his surroundings feeling unreal, a sensation that he tried desperately to fight off. He frequently reassured himself and thought about what he was experiencing. He would avoid walking past an old asylum that was on his normal route to work. He avoided reading any references in the media to madness.

Key aspects of Steven's recovery

At the beginning of his recovery, Steven used an 'ABA' experiment to clarify in his mind the effect of trying to control his thoughts and feelings that his surroundings were unreal. He soon discovered that the more he fought against these experiences the worse he found them. This helped him to become more accepting of his thoughts and feelings. Steven liked the idea of tackling his fears head on and arranged to visit a local psychiatric unit, which upon arrival he found extremely scary. He talked to patients who were recovering from schizophrenia. But to his surprise, after about an hour he noticed he felt very much calmer. To make his exposure more practical, he found as many films as he could that involved mental illness and watched the scenes he found most upsetting again and again until he felt bored with them. He visited the museum at the Bethlem Royal, one of the oldest psychiatric hospitals in the world. He then wrote out a story describing his worst fears happening, and read this each day for 20 minutes over a two-week period. He found this made it far easier for him to see his thoughts and images as mental events or 'just rubbish that pops into my head because I'm afraid of it'. He wrote and talked about some of his childhood experiences and was able to link some of the fears of losing control with his father.

Steven's avoidance and safety behaviors

Figure 9.4 Vicious flower: Steven's example

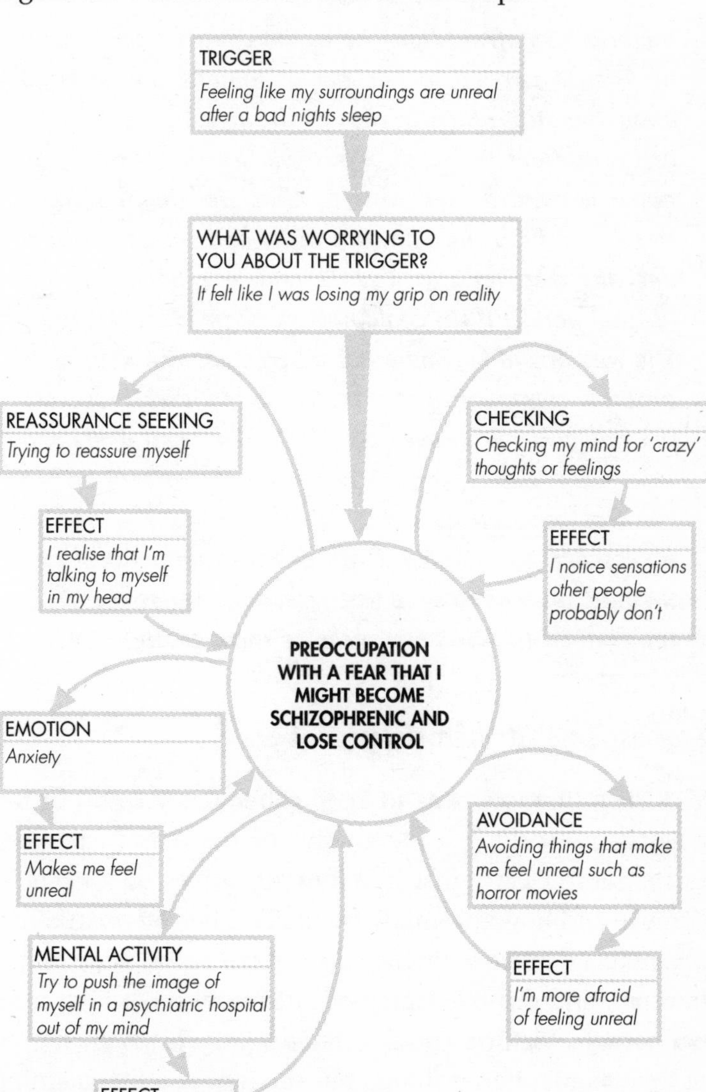

Victoria's preoccupation with a fear of blood borne illness

Victoria was afraid that she would contract some form of disease carried in her blood. Initially she worried about hepatitis and AIDS, but as she investigated further on the Internet, the scope of possible illnesses she worried about expanded. She worried that she might have a disease while being unaware of it, and that she would one day discover this disease and look back over his life and wonder if she could have performed much better. She was afraid he would not be treated with dignity or properly communicated with. She hated it when doctors did not give her proper feedback. She had a lifelong tendency to health anxiety that generally worsened when she was stressed for other reasons. When she was an adolescent, the sudden death of her grandmother and an aunt she was close to was relevant, in that she never understood the circumstances of their death.

Key aspects of Victoria's recovery

Victoria's first step was to keep a frequency count of her reassurance-seeking using a tally counter. This helped her to see more clearly just how often she was seeking reassurance and how this might be fuelling her preoccupation. She reduced and eventually stopped her researching on the Internet, and did the same with reassurance-seeking from her parents. Victoria also devoted a relatively small amount of time to attention-training, but she reported that learning to distance herself from her thoughts about disease was the technique she found the most useful. She also visited an HIV clinic in a local hospital as part of her exposure. She was very struck that although some of the people attending probably did have a blood-borne illness, none of them looked as worried as she did. This helped her to draw a clearer distinction between fear and illness – seeing that, even if you are ill, hours of worry each day is not inevitable. Earlier in her recovery she would say to herself that she was allowed to engage with thoughts about her health only once a week (which she soon discovered she was actually not that interested in doing), and then increased this to once a fortnight, then once a month. She began to re-engage with sports and fitness activities, and returned to full time work. She began to tolerate uncertainty and accepted that if she did have a serious illness she would communicate to her relatives and doctors how she would like to be treated.

Victoria's main avoidance and safety behaviors

Figure 9.5 Vicious flower: Victoria's example

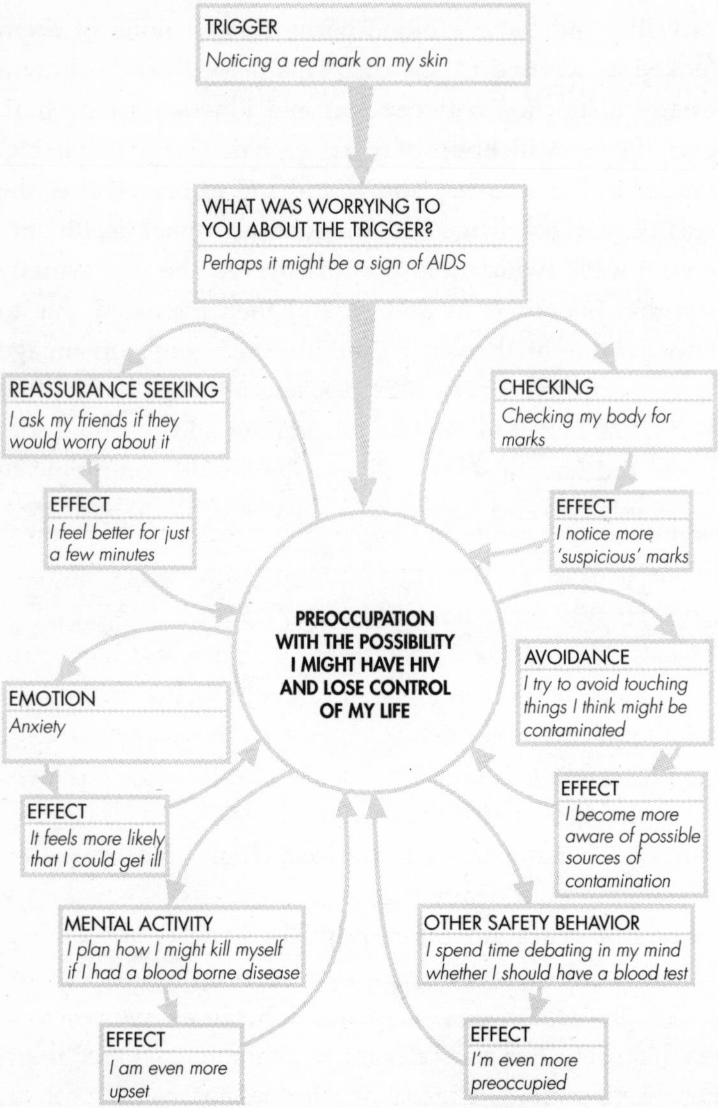

TRIGGER
Noticing a red mark on my skin

WHAT WAS WORRYING TO YOU ABOUT THE TRIGGER?
Perhaps it might be a sign of AIDS

PREOCCUPATION WITH THE POSSIBILITY I MIGHT HAVE HIV AND LOSE CONTROL OF MY LIFE

REASSURANCE SEEKING
I ask my friends if they would worry about it

EFFECT
I feel better for just a few minutes

CHECKING
Checking my body for marks

EFFECT
I notice more 'suspicious' marks

EMOTION
Anxiety

EFFECT
It feels more likely that I could get ill

AVOIDANCE
I try to avoid touching things I think might be contaminated

EFFECT
I become more aware of possible sources of contamination

MENTAL ACTIVITY
I plan how I might kill myself if I had a blood borne disease

EFFECT
I am even more upset

OTHER SAFETY BEHAVIOR
I spend time debating in my mind whether I should have a blood test

EFFECT
I'm even more preoccupied

10

Overcoming a fear of death

Fears about death are a common feature of health anxiety. This chapter may serve a number of purposes in helping you overcome health anxiety. It may help you to see how common thoughts and fears of death are experienced so that you learn you are not alone; it should give you some ideas on overcoming an excessive fear of death; and for some readers simply reading and re-reading this chapter will be an excellent way of confronting something that they may normally try to avoid thinking about.

Fears of death or dead things (e.g. corpses) have the grand name of 'necrophobia' or 'thanatophobia' (although these terms are not used by clinicians). Necrophobia also includes objects associated with death (e.g. coffins). Necrophobia is derived from the Greek *nekros* meaning 'corpse'. Thanatophobia is derived from 'Thanatos', the personification of death.

Fears of death are common in the general population and occur much more frequently in people with health anxiety. But fear of death can also occur in people without health anxiety. It is generally more common in women than men. Having strong religious beliefs does not seem to protect people from fears of death. The first step to understanding this particular fear is to determine the meaning behind it that drives your desire to avoid thinking about your own death.

Depression and suicide

This chapter is not suitable for you at this stage if you are very depressed and low mood has now become your main problem. If you wish to end your life, even if you have not made plans to do so, we strongly recommend that you seek help from your family doctor immediately. A family doctor will be able to offer you diagnosis and further treatment for your depression.

If you have self-harmed or considered self-harming, again it is advisable to seek help from your family doctor.

Taphephobia

A very specific fear is that of being buried alive (or 'taphephobia') and dying in one's coffin. This was a common fear in previous centuries. Like an obsession, it was characterized by many rituals – for example obtaining frequent reassurance and checking over the procedure at death. In the past, people would make very detailed instructions in their wills to ensure that they were not buried alive. They might request that their veins were cut or that they were buried in a coffin that could communicate to the surface by ringing a bell. Most people are now cremated and usually trust their doctors to correctly diagnose death. Reports of people having taking a drugs overdose and waking up in a mortuary are extremely rare. If tapehophobia is a problem for you, then the key issue is giving up your safety-seeking behaviors, learning to tolerate the doubt that you may be buried alive and living life to the full now.

Common beliefs about death

There are very many different types of beliefs that keep fear of death going, and here we will discuss some of the most common ones.

> *The process of dying is likely to be very painful and involve a lot of suffering.*

The experience of people who die from terminal illnesses find that they are well supported and that pain is reasonably well controlled. The issue for some people with a fear of death is the actual moment of dying. There have been reports of people who have died from a heart attack, for example, and then have been resuscitated, and who have later described death as an extremely pleasant process. This is probably because at the time of death the brain releases its own opiate drug (called endorphins) to give you a warm pleasant feeling, and so is not something to fear.

> *The afterlife may be an experience worse than living.*

You might believe that after death you will be a floating soul with thoughts and feelings, unable to control events around you. If you believe these thoughts and images to be an accurate prediction of the future (see a description of 'magical thinking' on page 10) then you are *fusing* them with past experiences and treating them as important as the here and now. Your thoughts and images are just mental events and have no power to predict the future – they just represent your fears. If you believe them, it's very understandable that you will do everything you can do to prevent yourself from dying. This is turn can become a preoccupation. You can be extremely self-focused and endlessly analysing and trying to know for certain what will happen when you die. This preoccupation and living in one's head means that you won't have a life now. However, it is equally likely that when you are dead you will have no thoughts or feelings, as you won't know about it.

My partner might marry someone I hate or my children won't cope without me as a parent.

This fear might take the form of an intrusive image. Death represents the ultimate in giving up control. Thus you may try to do everything you can to try to be in control of events after you die (and ruin your life now as everyone gets fed up with your antics in trying to control everything). It's true that your partner might get a life if you die and even your children will cope without you as others will rally around to support them. Equally, when you are dead your relatives and friends can dance on your grave if they wanted to and there's nothing you can do about it now! Your worries about what will happen if you die probably tell you more about your relationship with your partner or children now rather than what will happen after your death.

If you are experiencing thoughts or images about what will happen after you die then just try to experience them without engaging with them and without trying to control them. Do not try to run them on with a happy ending since this just maintains the fear. Read Chapter 3 again and keep acting in the directions that are important for you while you are alive.

I have doubts about what will happen after death.

People without strong religious beliefs may have the most difficulty with existential doubts about death. If you are religious you are likely to have faith in your teachings, although these do not necessarily protect you from fear – we have had many patients with doubts about the teachings of their faith. The problem here is the endless analysis and rumination involved in trying to find an answer. Each answer usually leads to more questions and doubts, leading to a vicious circle. There is of course no answer – if there were, someone would have worked it out before you. The best way of thinking about being dead is to think about what it was like before you were born. Enough said?

I might go to Hell.

This fear is a little like the existential doubt above about what will happen after death. You may benefit from talking to a minister of your religion about this issue. Hell is not so prominent these days in most religions and you will probably be told that where you go is not in your control. If you go to Hell, then you are very likely to find us there as well, so we can counsel you at the same time!

> *I should die at a reasonable old age and it would terrible and unfair to die any younger than this.*

People with health anxiety know that they have to die (although we have met a few people who believe in cryogenics), but the issue is usually not dying 'prematurely'. Unfortunately there is no law in the universe that says that you must die during old age. The average age of death may be about seventy-five for men and about seventy-nine for women, but this is an average: some people die much younger and some people die a bit older. The age of death is of course skewed so that people die from a vast range of ages from childbirth up to seventy-five and equally a number are then bunched up to die between seventy-five and about one hundred. By definition, an average means that you are just as likely to die under the age of seventy-five. Even if you follow a healthy lifestyle and there is longevity in your relatives you can be killed in an accident or develop some rare cancer through no fault of your own. Barring accidents, our genes probably largely decide our life expectancy. We ourselves have only a modest influence over when we die. We would of course encourage you to follow a healthy lifestyle (so long as the pursuit of a healthy lifestyle does not become excessive and means you don't have a life) *but* recognize that there are no rules about whether you should die at an old age. You may or you may not die young – you have a limited influence over the time and date of your death. Overcoming this fear is, again, about giving up control in your mind.

Consequences of a fear of death

If you fear death then there are usually two main consequences. The first is that you are likely to avoid triggers that remind you of the idea of your own death. The second is that you may be trying too hard to prevent yourself from dying. These include safety-seeking behaviors that are common in health anxiety. The next sections deal specifically with avoidance of images and ideas about your death. Whereas most phobias are very unlikely to happen, we can say for certain that death will happen – it's just that we don't know when. Unlike other fears, you can't overcome your fear or test out your predictions about death by ending your life (or at least this is not a solution we would advocate!). There are many better alternatives that will allow you to eventually experience the thoughts, ideas or images about your death without distress. The secret of life is to live in the moment without making any judgement. The trick is not to focus on what you could have experienced in the past, trying to find reasons for past experiences or what you might experience in the future. Invariably if you fear and worry about death, it leads you to avoid life. These processes will ruin your experience of the present and interfere with your valued directions in life.

EXERCISES

This section should be read after you have read about the principles of exposure and behavioral experiments to test out your predictions (see Chapter 7). You will recall that worry often leads to inactivity and avoidance of actions that you take to prepare yourself for what is likely. Death is about the only guarantee in life and there are many exercises you can do to prepare for the 'Grim Reaper'. Note that some family members or friends may have their own issues relating to death so don't be surprised if they are unenthusiastic about your doing any of these exercises or think that we (the authors) are just sick. But these exercises really can help with fears of death!

1 Seek inspirational role models who have accepted death gracefully, or have used the news that they are going to die to motivate themselves to get the most from their lives in their final months. Randy Pausch's 'Last Lecture' (on childhood dreams) for instance, which can easily be found on the Internet, is a truly inspirational example of someone who has come to terms with the fact that he is dying from cancer and has only months to live.
2 Make your will. This will help you to contemplate your own death – and is important to do even if you don't have a fear of death! If you don't make a will and fall under a bus tomorrow the government will decide how your estate is to be divided up (which you may not like). The way of dividing up your estate differs from country to country but if you leave it up to the government you will not be able, for example, to

leave any of your money to a charity for research into health anxiety. Make sure you appoint two executors to ensure your wishes are carried out. You may also make other wishes about a guardian for any children or whom you would like them to be looked after by. Make sure that you write your will assuming you will die tomorrow and review it when your circumstances change.

3 Write your obituary or eulogy for your own funeral. This is not actually as ridiculous as it sounds. Doctors are encouraged to write their own obituaries for the British Medical Journal and to keep it up to date like a curriculum vitae that they write for job applications. An advantage of writing your own obituary is that you can make sure your record is accurate. It is then an enormous help to your executor or relative who will have to tell your mourners about your life and what it stood for. It doesn't of course mean that the person who gives your eulogy or writes an obituary doesn't put a different slant on your life. For your purpose of overcoming your fear of death, when you write the obituary make sure that it reads as if you died tomorrow. Write in detail about your life and what you strove for. Tell your executor where you have filed the details about your life and discuss it with a close relative or friend.

4 Write out and discuss your wishes for your funeral arrangements. Do you want an ecological funeral? There are many ways of disposing of bodies that are better for the environment than burial. Do you have any wishes about being buried or cremated? If cremated, what will you like done with your ashes? Again, discussing your wishes and writing them down

is important. Even if you don't have a fear of death, if you fail to discuss your wishes then your relatives may do something you are not happy with. For example, they might arrange a semi-religious funeral in an expensive coffin when you are an atheist and want a biodegradable coffin – or vice versa!

You might want to discuss some of the music that you'd like to have played or the literature to be read. One of us has every intention of asking our children to annoy a few of our relatives with a live jazz band and some John Coltrane – such a shame that we won't be alive to appreciate it! We have also requested for our ashes to be donated to our clinic so they can be kept in the cupboard and taken out for exposure tasks and behavioral experiments for people with a fear of death and health anxiety. No doubt Health and Safety might have something to say about this, but so much better to overcome your fears of death with the ashes of the authors of the chapter you are reading! It gives a whole new meaning to interactive media. So if you want to donate your ashes to helping other people suffering from health anxiety, or sprinkle them in the River Ganges or shoot them to the stars, write down your preferences and wishes about your final party (and make sure you leave money to pay for it!). This exercise will again help you to think about your own mortality but it is also a very normal activity.

5 Throw an anti-necrophobia (or anti-fear of death) party. Again, this is not as ridiculous as it sounds. One of us recently had his fiftieth birthday and does not particularly like growing old – we all have our issues! He therefore threw a party that celebrated death with the most fun possible. There was a Grim

Reaper and someone else dressed as the Devil to welcome guests. We had an actor who played a funeral director who kindly measured people up for a coffin and discussed their wishes. There was even a coffin in the garden to try out. One of the band's numbers was to improvise on the Funeral March. After dinner chocolates consisted of 'Obols' to be put under one's tongue to pay the ferryman, Charon, to take guests across the mythical River Hades in the garden. All the guests reported having a good time, although we fear some of the people who did not attend may have been very superstitious. We are sure you can think of many equally fun exercises to overcome a fear of death whilst having a good party!

6 Expose yourself to specific triggers that remind you of death. There may be many different triggers. You might avoid:

- taking a route that passes a cemetery
- funerals
- reading obituaries or deaths in the media
- watching movies or TV programs that involve death or dying
- reading books about people are dying or have died
- discussing death
- having a pet (which some people avoid as pets often die before their owners).

All these need to be added to your hierarchy (see page 143) for exposure and done repeatedly until fear is no longer associated with each of these triggers. You can add to your hierarchy to look at personifications of death like the 'Grim Reaper' or putting up pictures of Hell in your bedroom; visit a grave or memorial stone of someone in the family; visit a funeral parlour; read the accounts and blogs of people suffering from terminal illnesses and who eventually die. Death is not something most of us want to happen but the issue is learning not to fear it and not allowing yourself to experience the intrusive thoughts and feelings about death.

7 Write a story about your own death. Write it in the first person and in the present tense as if it is happening now from an field perspective (that is through your own eyes rather than observing yourself). Write a step-by-step account using as many different senses as possible (what you see, what you feel, what you hear, what you smell). Be sure to focus on your specific fears (suffocating, for instance) and that it finishes at your death (and not an afterlife).

8 Have you had any experiences of death connected with a close relative or friend that have been traumatic or bad? This would make your fears very understandable and likely to be still influencing the present. If there are aspects of their death you are avoiding then you may benefit from seeing a therapist to talk through these issues or use imagery to re-experience them and understand some of the meaning that is linked to your relative's or friend's death. This may be contributing to some of the beliefs and feelings that you have now and may be keeping your fear going.

11

Overcoming a fear of vomiting

A specific phobia of vomiting is a condition that is often misunderstood and regarded as difficult to overcome. However, it is treatable and this chapter aims to help you understand the phobia – its causes, effects and the principles of how you can overcome it. We have included this chapter here because a phobia of vomiting overlaps with that of health anxiety in terms of excessive worrying, checking and avoidance behaviors.

The common name for a specific phobia of vomiting is emetophobia. It is a condition where an individual fears vomiting him- or herself or fears others vomiting. If you have emetophobia, you may equally fear vomiting alone or in public. You may frequently experience *feeling* sick but you are probably no more at risk of being sick than most people who do not go out and get drunk or than someone eating foods of a type wholly unfamiliar to them. Neither of the authors have vomited for between twenty and thirty years each and yet we have taken no special precautions to stop ourselves from vomiting.

Fear of vomiting may have become a preoccupation for you and the main thing you think about. Vomiting is associated with overwhelming fear and panic. Some people fear losing control, becoming very ill or that others will find them repulsive. Most people with emetophobia are afraid of themselves vomiting, and of others to a lesser extent. Mostly the fear of others relates to the fear they may catch something from them, or it reminds them of vomiting – very few emetophobics are exclusively concerned with the fear of others vomiting. Whatever the focus of vomiting, you are likely to try too hard to avoid a wide range of situations, foods, drinks and activities that you believe might increase a risk of vomiting.

Vomiting upsets many people, but to be diagnosed with a specific phobia of vomiting must be very distressing and interfere with your life in important ways. For example, it may interfere with an important relationship or your social life. It may prevent you from a desired pregnancy or you may be unhealthily underweight. You may not be able to go on holiday or travel on public transport.

Coping with emetophobia

If you have emetophobia, you are probably avoiding a range of activities or situations. These can usually be divided into:

a) Avoiding adults or children who could be ill (and regarded as contagious) or who may be at risk of vomiting (e.g. drunks who remind you of vomiting). The avoidance might extend to restricting activities of any children who may be in contact with other children.

b) Avoiding situations or activities that present a higher risk of vomiting such as going on holiday abroad; places where you may see drunks; visiting sick people; travelling by boat or aeroplane; drinking alcohol in normal amounts; crowded places; using public transport; pregnancy; fairground rides; using public toilets or door handles; medication; going to the dentist; anaesthesia. Women with babies might experience a great deal of distress about their child vomiting and want to escape from their child.
c) Avoiding food. Food restriction may occur in a variety of ways:
   i) Restricting the amount of food eaten that reaches your stomach, thus reducing the amount that might be vomited. Alternatively a restricted amount is equated with feeling 'full', since continuing to eat once you feel you've had enough could lead to vomiting.
   ii) Restricting food in certain contexts (for example, not eating food cooked by someone else or in an unfamiliar restaurant).
   iii) Restricting certain types of food (for example, shellfish, poultry, curries, dairy products and fried fast food) that might have a slightly higher risk of inducing vomiting. Alternatively, certain foods may have become associated with a past experience of vomiting.

Restricting food may lead to being very underweight, which may have a number of physiological consequences and be a further factor in increasing anxiety and nausea.

You may also have a number of 'safety-seeking behaviors'. These are things you do that you believe will prevent yourself or others from being sick. These include:

- excessive checking of sell-by dates and the freshness of food
- seeking reassurance
- excessive cooking of food
- excessive washing of hands
- excessive cleaning of the kitchen area with anti-bacterial sprays and gels; superstitious behaviors such as 'not stepping on a 13th stair'
- repeating a word or action a certain number to prevent yourself from vomiting
- taking anti-nausea medication
- sucking antacids, ice or mints
- frequently drinking bottled water or a sugar fizzy drink. This may also be a way of checking whether you are going to be sick (e.g. 'If water's going down, then nothing can come up').

You might also be telling yourself certain things in your head, such as reassuring yourself that you or someone else will not be sick. Even though it's impossible, you may attempt to mentally control the reflex act of vomiting.

All these avoidance, safety-seeking behaviors and being extra-vigilant keep the problem going. They appear to work (in the sense that you do not vomit) but have the unintended consequence of increasing your awareness of feeling sick. They make you more preoccupied with vomiting and more anxious. This becomes a vicious circle as you feel more nauseous and so on. In short, it is your solutions that have become the problem and are now keeping the fear going.

The cause of emetophobia

We don't know what causes emetophobia but some people may be more genetically predisposed to developing it than others. It is intriguing that emetophobia is much more likely to occur in women. Men with emetophobia are very uncommon.

Developing a specific phobia of vomiting is highly understandable given the way that humans (and animals) can become easily conditioned after food poisoning or an infection and are more likely to avoid situations that remind them of vomiting. Vomiting as a baby or as a child can be panic-inducing (for example, by making associations with the feeling of suffocating, choking or death). Even if as an adult you know these associations are not valid, they are still powerfully linked in your mind. However, these associations can also be unlearnt and the 'ghosts of the past' can change.

Specific phobias (such as insects, heights) are relatively common and occur in about 10 per cent of the population. It is important to differentiate anxiety or disgust of vomiting (which is very common) from a specific phobia of vomiting (which is relatively uncommon). In very large surveys of specific phobias, only one study asked about a phobia of vomiting; and this phobia was found to be relatively uncommon, affecting 0.1 per cent of the population. However, it's hard to say exactly how many people have a specific phobia of vomiting since some may be misdiagnosed as having obsessive-compulsive disorder or health anxiety. Many people with emetophobia are too ashamed to talk about their problem. It is nonetheless agreed that specific phobias of vomiting are generally more handicapping than other specific phobias and are more difficult to treat.

Emetophobia may be linked to other conditions. You may feel demoralized or clinically depressed. Some people restrict their food believing that a range of food may cause vomiting. You may then become very underweight, which is why some people with emetophobia are misdiagnosed with anorexia nervosa and are treated inappropriately. No long-term follow-up studies have been done. Many people with emetophobia have a chronic condition. If left untreated, the condition is likely to persist.

If you have emetophobia, you might be asking yourself 'Why do humans and animals have to vomit? Vomiting is an adaptive process that increases your chances of survival if you are ill. If you are infected, vomiting is beneficial and prevents disease by getting rid of toxins. Do you know the rat is the only animal that cannot vomit? This is one reason why rat poison is so effective. Try to view your ability to vomit as protecting you. If you couldn't vomit , then you'd be more prone to illnesses.

Perceptions of vomiting

Some people with emetophobia believe that if vomiting does occur it will last for many days. In fact, after an infection or food poisoning, it usually lasts at the most a day or two.

Others believe that they can influence or control their vomiting in an almost magical way. But as we have seen, the act of vomiting is a primitive reflex act. There is no evidence that you can stop yourself from vomiting – if you are going to vomit you will vomit. It might feel as if you have stopped yourself from vomiting, but in reality in such instances you would not have vomited in the first place. People with emetophobia tend to focus on the risk of infection or food poisoning, but the reflex can be triggered by a wide variety of triggers around the body (including mechanically in gynaecological problems; a extremely stretched gall-bladder or stomach; by certain drugs; metabolic problems that act on the brain stem; extreme fear; severe pain; certain smells can all induce vomiting in the right context).

Treatments available

There has been very little research on the best treatment for emetophobia. Anti-nausea medication is often prescribed at the request of people with emetophobia. Yet this doesn't solve the problem and is usually unhelpful in the long term as it reinforces the idea that you can control vomiting and the idea that vomiting must be avoided at all costs. We suspect that anti-nausea medication acts as a placebo.

There is no evidence that psychiatric medication is of any benefit in emetophobia. On the other hand, there is a rationale for a type of medication called a selective serotonergic reuptake inhibitor (SSRI) in those with severe symptoms that overlap with health anxiety and obsessive compulsive disorder (OCD) and who have not got better with CBT. This is described in more detail in Chapter 15. Nausea is a potential side effect of a SSRI, which may mean that it is an unacceptable approach for some.

There is a lot of evidence for the benefit of cognitive behavior therapy (CBT) in other phobias and health anxiety. CBT can be adapted for treating a specific phobia of vomiting. You may have experienced CBT in the past that has not been helpful but its success may depend on who is delivering it and therefore the approach used. There is no evidence in the scientific literature for the benefit of hypnotherapy in emetophobia (other than one case report).

There are no miracle cures for emetophobia – overcoming the condition is hard work on the part of the individual with emetophobia. Having emetophobia can make life very restricted and part of your therapy will focus on helping you to do what is important in your life despite your fears. Over time the degree of distress and preoccupation with vomiting will decrease and your life will become more manageable. There are no risks or side effects of CBT other than the experience of anxiety and having old memories.

Self-help

As illustrated in this book, CBT consists of a structured program of self-help, enabling you to get a good understanding of how the fear might have developed and how your solutions have now become your problem and keep the fear going. It is based on an understanding that people with emetophobia have had one or more bad experience of vomiting from childhood. Sometimes such an experience can be remembered, sometimes not. These memories have become associated with fear. Past experiences of vomiting (and their triggers) become fused with the present so that they are re-experienced *as if* they are about to be repeated. Once the link with the past experience is learnt, the anticipation of vomiting leads to anxiety. However, anxiety also causes nausea and other stomach symptoms. This becomes linked to the idea of vomiting and losing control. This in turn is associated with extreme fear and past experiences of vomiting, leading to a vicious circle.

There are then various ways that people with emetophobia then cope with the idea of vomiting. These are not bizarre – it is a very natural and understandable response to fear.

a) You may try to avoid thoughts and images of yourself or others vomiting and feelings of nausea.
b) You are more vigilant than the average person in monitoring threats (for example people who could be ill or an escape route).
c) You become excessively self-focused in order to monitor nausea.

d) You worry, try to reassure yourself and mentally plan escape routes from others who might vomit.
e) You may think in a 'magical way' and try to 'neutralize' thoughts and images of vomiting in a way that you believe will stop you from vomiting.
f) You may use safety-seeking behaviors including compulsive checking and reassurance-seeking.

All these ways of coping make you *feel* that you have more control in your ability to stop yourself from vomiting or that you are doing something to reduce uncertainty. However, they will have the unintended consequence of increasing your preoccupation and frequency of thoughts about vomiting and symptoms of nausea and make you more anxious, leading you into a vicious circle.

What you can do

The first step is to analyse the problem from the perspective above to gain an understanding of what is keeping the problem going and to use the information from Chapter 2. The solution therefore involves some combination of:

a) gradually dropping your avoidance and safety-seeking behaviors using the principles of exposure (see Chapter 7). This includes allowing yourself to experience thoughts and images about yourself and others vomiting. You should not be asked to induce vomiting – this is not necessary. But it will be important, for example, to deliberately enter situations that you avoid, and do some exposure in your imagination to yourself vomiting or other people being sick.

b) Refocusing your attention externally and to stop checking for people who might be ill (see Chapter 6).
c) Understanding your motivation in worrying about vomiting and not engaging with your intrusive thoughts or images (see Chapter 5).
d) Questioning the magical thinking and excessive responsibility in believing you can influence your vomiting. The key issue is acceptance of the idea that one day you might vomit (see Chapter 4).
e) It may also be helpful update your early memories and images of vomiting so they are no longer viewed as relevant now. This is usually done with a trained therapist.

We shall now describe the process as experienced by an individual with emetophobia. Nicki had suffered from an excessive fear of being sick since she was eleven years old. She could recall waking up one night and suddenly violently vomiting all over her bedroom floor. At the time she felt helpless and it felt like an age before managed to call her mother to her bedroom. She wondered if this particular moment of being sick gained particular significance in her mind as she had just started attending senior school. Her main way of coping until she sought help was to keep the range and quantity of foods very restricted. This had left her looking thin and pale. Although there were frequent rows at home about this, ultimately her parents became defeated and accommodated her special eating habits.

Nicki's main reason for seeking help, at age twenty-four, was because she was in a long-term relationship and hoped that they would eventually have a child. Her partner complained regularly about the fact that the could never go out for a meal together, let alone go to a pub or even the cinema because of Nicki's fears of someone being sick or catching a bug. She was still slightly underweight. She became extremely preoccupied by watching for reports in the media about a norovirus that causes stomach upsets, and she had a friend who also had a vomit phobia whom she frequently talked with and gave reassurance about not vomiting.

Nicki began her recovery by drawing up a list of the things she did excessively or avoided because of her fear of vomiting and nausea. This was shown in the diagram opposite.

She saw a cognitive behavior therapist and agreed to tackle her problem 'as if' it was a problem of fear, rather than a problem of being imminently sick. With the support of her partner, she steadily dropped each of her safety-seeking behaviors and gradually faced up to situations. She gradually reintroduced the foods she avoided and the amount that she ate so she began to reach a normal weight. She stopped constantly drinking bottled water.

Whenever she was in social situations and after eating she made a concerted effort to focus her attention on to the world around her, rather than monitoring the sensations in her body (for example the feelings of nausea) or whether

Figure 11.1 Vicious flower: Nicki's example

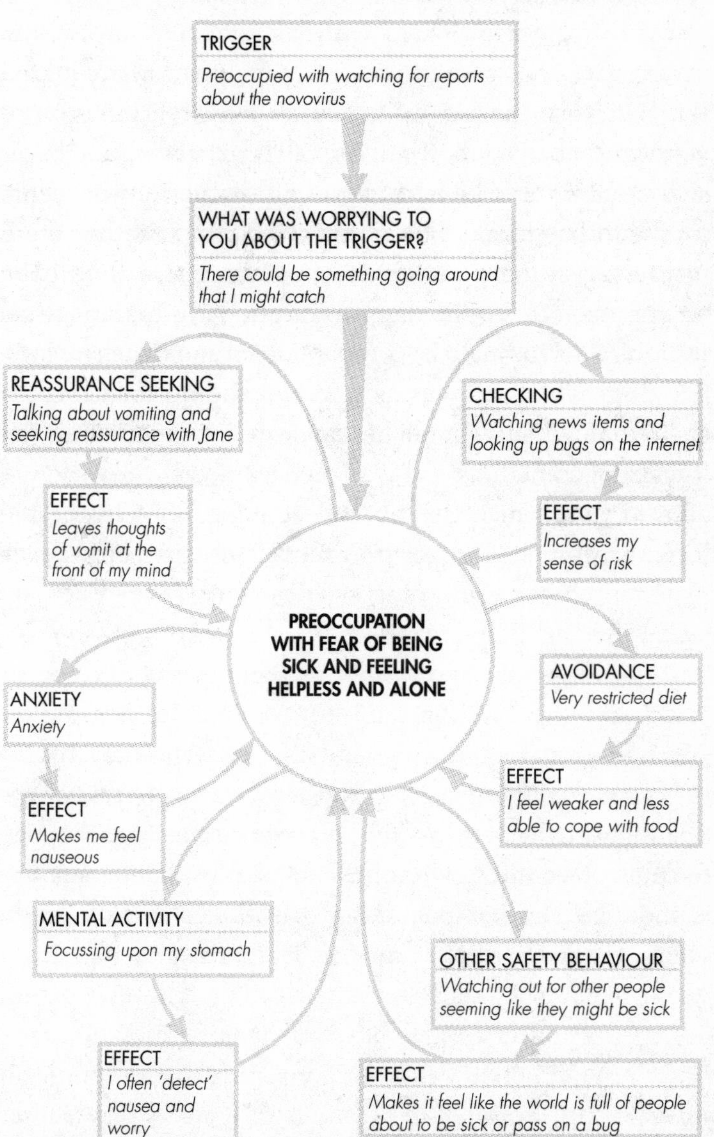

other people looked as if they might be feeling ill. When she experienced intrusive images of being sick then she learnt to experience them without repeating any mantra that she was not going to be sick. She learnt to accept that she had very limited influence on her ability to control vomiting and eventually gave up all her checking and excessive monitoring. She had to ban all discussions of feeling sick with her friend. She found it helpful with her therapist to revisit the experiences of vomiting as a child using an approach called 'imagery rescripting'. In her image she was able as an adult to be compassionate and caring towards her child when she was sick. When she finished therapy, she remained still somewhat anxious about vomiting, but it was not something she was preoccupied by and she was able to function in her normal activities. She eventually took the plunge, and got pregnant. During pregnancy she experienced some morning sickness but was not actually sick. When her daughter was born, she had normal illnesses such as diarrhoea and vomiting. This was a big test for Nicki and she had some top-up sessions in therapy. But she managed to care for her baby appropriately by not escaping or ringing up her partner to come to rescue her. She allowed herself to fully experience the thoughts and feelings of vomiting without trying to distract herself and without refusing to look at her baby. Later in the year she went on holiday abroad for the first time.

12

Overcoming depression

Health anxiety can be a tough problem to live with and as a result some sufferers become depressed. In addition, depression can fuel worries about one's health. Indeed, in certain cultures and amongst the elderly, complaints about body sensations can be the primary symptoms reported when the person suffers from depression. Common body sensations and changes that occur in depression include:

- feeling fatigued
- sleep disturbance
- changes in sex drive
- changes in appetite
- headaches
- constipation
- aches and pains

So if your mood has been low in addition to your feeling anxious it might be very helpful to consider depression as a possible cause of physical or mental sensations. Depression also makes our minds much more likely to generate negative thoughts and images. The other critical effect that depression can have is to make a person become far more receptive to negative information. Thus if a negative thoughts or image (e.g. an image of yourself ill, or of your funeral) crosses your mind, low mood may be one of the reasons. Again, it is worth considering this as an alternative to believing that the image must be important or a sign that the picture in your mind will come true. People with health anxiety and severe depression should seek help immediately if they feel suicidal or have strange beliefs (for example that their body is rotting or that they have cancer, when they don't). Sometimes people believe that they would be better off dead so that their relatives do not have to cope with their suffering from an alleged illness like cancer.

This chapter describes a key CBT strategy in overcoming depression – it is called 'behavioral activation' (BA). By focusing on the effect of what you do, you will gain an understanding of how best to choose activities that bring lasting improvement in your mood and make your life more satisfying. Much of this chapter is taken from our book *Manage Your Mood,* which has a lot more detailed advice on overcoming depression. You may also wish to read another book in this series, *Overcoming Depression* by Paul Gilbert.

The assumptions of the therapy are that depression is a consequence of avoiding or trying to control unpleasant thoughts, feelings and pictures in you mind and trying to find reasons for what has happened in the past. This can easily be applied to health anxiety as you try harder to avoid or control unpleasant feelings. The effect is that you become inactive and withdrawn, and you miss out on experiences in life that you normally find rewarding. In addition, if you begin to neglect yourself, your home and your relationships you will find that life begins to feel worse. This easily occurs in health anxiety since you avoid more because of your fears of illness.

What are you avoiding?

The first step is to consider what you are avoiding at present. Below is a list of activities that are most commonly avoided or done excessively by people who are depressed. Read the statements and tick the ones that apply to you. When you tick an item, think of a specific example and analyse the action. Think of a specific situation in which it was relevant and work out the immediate effect and the unintended effect on yourself, others and the environment around you. Later in this chapter you will use this information to plan your activities.

COGNITIVE AND BEHAVIORAL AVOIDANCE CHECKLIST	
I avoid social activities	
I make excuses not to attend social events	
I ignore the phone and texts or emails from friends	
I limit myself to events where the people are familiar	
I tell myself that I prefer to be alone	
I leave social gatherings early	

I keep myself to myself or stick to someone I know at a social gathering	
I avoid socializing with the sex to which I am attracted	
I have reduced or stopped my leisure activities (e.g. visiting pub, cinema, theatre, club, restaurant, gallery, football match)	
I have reduced or stopped solo hobbies (e.g. fishing, playing a musical instrument, DIY, reading, painting, gardening, running)	
I do not take as much care of myself as I used to (e.g. washing, hair care, regular clean clothes and sheets)	
I have reduced or stopped paying attention to my role as a parent/partner/son or daughter	
I have reduced time spent cooking and have been living on junk food	
I have given up tidying or cleaning my home	
I have stopped opening or replying to letters, and paying bills	
Instead of acting as a good student or employee, I accept what I think are my limits at school or at work	
I am not following up what I want to achieve at college or work	
I am sticking with the things I know rather than developing new interests (whether at college or work or in my spare time), in which I may fail	
I quit activities early where I feel that they are too challenging, even though others do not agree with me	
I try not to think about problems in any of my relationships but just let things go on as they are	
I do not think about what I really want in life	
I avoid communicating with my partner/parents/children	
I am not getting serious about college or work	

I am trying to find a reason for the way I feel	
I am constantly thinking about why I acted in the past in the way I did	
I am trying to answer 'What if?' questions in my mind	
I am turning down opportunities to further my education or career	
I am fantasizing 'If only' situations (e.g. 'If only I had not acted in the way I did' or 'If only such and such had not happened')	
I avoid making important decisions about my future	
I distract myself when I think about work or education, or my role as parent or partner	
The following are relevant only when you do them excessively to stop yourself thinking or to numb yourself emotionally or to avoid doing something else	
I comfort-eat or binge-eat	
I watch TV	
I listen to music	
I spend time on the computer/Internet	
I drink alcohol	
I stay in bed in the morning or have frequent naps in the day	
I exercise excessively	
I use illegal substances	

Source: Questionnaire reproduced with permission from Canadian psychologists Nicole Ottenbreit and Keith Dobson.

Using an activity schedule

The next step is to find out exactly what you do in your everyday life and how long each activity takes. You may be surprised to find out how much of what you do is automatic or habitual.

An activity schedule is a timetable of your activities during a particular time period – an afternoon, a day, a week, or even several weeks – which is useful for recording what you do, understanding the effects of your activities, and planning and structuring for the future. Using your activity schedule you may:

- Record your current level of activity and use it for reference as you build up your activation.
- Record what you are doing and then review the extent to which you are 'stuck' in a narrowed range of activities. (Are you avoiding some activities and overdoing others?). Are there habits you have that might be maintaining your depression?
- Understand the extent to which your behavior reflects what is important to you. To what extent does your activity schedule reflect your valued directions in life?

Use the activity schedule below over the next few days to keep a detailed record of what you do and how long it takes. Then link each activity to how you were feeling at the time. Rate the severity of your depression on a simple scale between 0 and 10, where 0 is 'not depressed at all', and 10 is 'extremely depressed'. The chart does not have to be 'perfect' but it will help you if you can manage to fill in some details. Copies of the activity schedule that can be photocopied can be found in Appendix 3.

Analysing the results

Now bring together the results of all your analyses and activity schedules.

- **Review your avoidance checklist:** This provides an overview of the activities that you are avoiding, not taking seriously or are doing excessively. Now consider alternatives to what you are avoiding or to activities such as ruminating and watching excessive amounts of TV which serve to avoid what is important in your life.
- **Review your activity schedule over the past few days:** Can you now identify situations, activities, thoughts or feelings that you are avoiding or trying to escape from or to control, which keep you feeling depressed? How does your recorded activity level compare with your perception of it? Are you more productive than you realized, or are you be doing more or less of a particular activity than you had thought?
- **Review your 'valued directions' form.** What activities that are important to you have been set aside? And what activities do you want to introduce or do more of?
- **What pleasurable activities are you missing out on?** These could either be activities that you used

EXERCISE 12.1: DAILY ACTIVITY SCHEDULE

Day/date:

Time	Activity	Time	Activity
7 am		4 pm	
8 am		5 pm	
9 am		6 pm	
10 am		7 pm	
11 am		8 pm	
12 pm		9 pm	
1 pm		10 pm	
2 pm		11 pm	
3 pm		12 am	

to enjoy or that soothe you. Soothing activities might include having a long bath; having a massage; walking in a wood or along the beach; taking in pleasant smells; drawing or painting; listening to your favourite music; listening to a recording of the sound of water falling, birds at sunrise, or sounds in a jungle; going to a spa for the day; or doing random acts of kindness for others.

Planning your activities and setting goals

You should now have a good idea of your own patterns of avoidance, escape and control and what you are missing out on in life. We want you to make a detailed list of goals incorporating activities that:

- relate to the problems that you identified in Chapter 3
- you have cut down on or avoided since you became depressed. Remember 'activities' includes making decisions or planning (e.g. thinking about the steps you need to take to improve your education or career)
- you would like to start or do more of because they are important to you
- are alternatives to activities that you wish to limit or stop (e.g. excessive drinking, sleeping, comfort-eating, exercise and illegal drugs).

Start with short-term goals, which are easier to tackle, and set yourself a realistic timetable by which you intend to move on to the next set of goals. Try to identify one or two goals from the activities you have avoided and that are in your valued directions and introduce them on a daily basis. A good rule of thumb is to try to revert to how you used to behave before you developed depression *but in a gradual manner*. Your list should help you to follow your valued directions in life as you leave behind your habits of avoidance and excessive control.

You will probably find that some activities in your medium term will need breaking down into smaller steps. They may also require more forward planning – for example, a visit to a concert in a few weeks' time might involve booking a babysitter, getting tickets and agreeing where and when to meet up with a friend. Long-term goals (for example, getting a new job) may require a number of detailed steps (such as preparing your CV, reading advertisements and talking to a career counsellor or someone in a personnel department). All these elements need to be part of your goals and your plan.

The next step is to put these goals and activities into your planed timetable. Start with the short-term goals and act as if you have a series of appointments that you have to keep so that you do not let yourself down. You might also need to bring order to the chaos of your eating and sleeping habits by timetabling roughly when you plan to get up, buy food, cook and eat.

All this may seem overwhelming at first, but we have emphasized the importance of *gradually* introducing new activities that you have previously avoided or that are in your valued directions.

The golden rules of behavioral activation

If your behavioral activation is to work, you will need to follow these guiding principles.

1 Build up gradually from where you are now; don't ruminate on what you 'should' be doing

Don't focus on all the things you think you *should* be doing, as this often leads to an overwhelmingly long list. Instead, choose your activities carefully and aim for small changes to begin with, building up the level of activity gradually.

2 Relate your plan to your analysis

Don't fill your day with activity just for activities sake. Make sure your activities relate to what will help you feel more on top of things and activities that will bring you degrees of pleasure and satisfaction. Try to act in accordance with your valued directions in life. After completing a difficult task, reward yourself with activities that are soothing and pleasurable.

3 Incorporate a range of activities

It might, for example, be beneficial to set a time to get up each day to help regulate your sleep. You might also need to schedule in rest periods, which do not involve going to bed and sleeping, to help you gradually build up stamina.

Planning what, when and where to eat might help you to build a healthier eating pattern. You should include a full spectrum of activities in your activity schedule to help yourself become physically and psychologically healthier, and get your life on course in the directions you prefer. Fill in exercise 12.2 overleaf.

Carrying out your plan

1 Focus on the moment

As you undertake each activity, focus on the moment and the process of what you are doing. If your mind wants to chatter away negatively, just notice it and thank your mind but don't buy into the thoughts. For example, if you are cleaning and tidying your home, it's better to focus your attention on moving the vacuum cleaner around and the dirt being vacuumed, rather than listening to yourself saying, 'This place is such a mess' or 'If people could see how I've let things go, they'd be so shocked'. Experience the world as it is now, rather than the way you think it is.

2 Don't let your thoughts get in the way

Your mind will tell you that there's no point in trying anything because: a) you won't enjoy it; b) you'll be humiliated and make a fool of yourself; c) nothing you can do will make any difference; or d) you'll end up feeling worse. Expect this from your mind and quietly ignore your mental chatter. Feeling as if you've no 'get-up and go', coupled with a sense of 'what's the point', is a typical experience when you are suffering from depression. Buying into your thoughts for being 'vulnerable' or 'good for nothing' only serves to worsen the problem by lowering your mood and leading to inactivity. You may want to re-read Chapter 3 to understand how you may be fusing your thoughts with reality.

3 Stay supportive

Activity can be difficult when you are depressed and feeling ashamed of your body. You'll find that you still have 'bad' (less active) days on your journey towards reclaiming your life. But try to act like an encouraging friend or trainer, rather than a negative and unhelpful critic. Acknowledge the pain in your life. Life can be full of suffering but even more important is how we respond to it.

4 Keep planning

Keep planning on a daily, weekly and monthly basis. Even if you don't stick entirely to your plan, you can get yourself back on track, rather than giving up on your plan because you experience thoughts like 'I've blown it so I might as well go back to bed!' Label this as a thought that you can quietly thank your mind for and then ignore.

Monitoring the effect of your scheduled activities

As you go through the week, note on your activity schedule exactly what you did (including deviations from your plan).

1 Rate what emotions were associated with each activity, marking the intensity from 0 to 10 (where 0 is 'not at all distressing' and 10 is 'extreme distress').

EXERCISE 12.2: PLANNED ACTIVITY SCHEDULE

Day/date:

Time	Planned activity	Actual activity	What was the effect of what I did on my emotions or the context in which I live?	Did it contribute towards my goals and valued directions in life? Rate it from 0–10 where 0 is not at all and 10 is extremely
7 am				
8 am				
9 am				
10 am				
11 am				
12 pm				
1 pm				
2 pm				

3 pm				
4 pm				
5 pm				
6 pm				
7 pm				
8 pm				
9 pm				
10 pm				
11 pm				
12–7 am				

2 Recognize how much the action contributes towards your goals and your valued directions in life. Evaluate the effect on yourself, on those around you and on your environment. Rate the action on a scale between 0 and 10 (where 0 is 'it did not contribute at all' and 10 is 'it contributed in full').

This will help you to:

- see an increased range in your behaviors
- appreciate changes in your mood
- assess areas that you are still avoiding or activities you are still over-using to block out problematic or painful thoughts.

Mental activities in depression

Brooding or self-attacking can lead to a number of unintended consequences, such as:

- feeling more depressed
- thinking more about bad events from the past
- believing thoughts in which you put yourself down
- being more pessimistic about the future
- being less able to generate effective solutions to problems and less confident in the ones you do generate
- becoming more withdrawn and doing less of what is important to you

- becoming more likely to be ignored and criticized by others
- being more likely to buy into the catastrophic and negative thoughts and images your health anxiety produces.

Brooding and ruminating

We described in Chapter 1 how people often have 'dark' thoughts or images when they feel depressed. However, brooding is different and describes a reaction to an intrusive thought or image. It may also be described as 'rumination'. Sometimes thinking about a difficulty can be productive and creative in terms of trying to solve an actual problem. However, it is not productive when someone is brooding, since this involves thinking excessively about past events or questions that cannot be resolved. It involves trying to find reasons for the situation you are in. People brood because they are attempting to solve problems by trying to figure things out from the past.

Brooding tends to focus on the past, with 'Why?' types of question, for example: 'Why did I smoke in the past?', or 'Why was I born this way?' There are variations on this theme, including fantasy thinking, which starts with 'If only'. For example: 'If only I could pull myself together', 'If only I could turn the clock back', 'If only I'd taken better care of my health'.

Spot when, where and how often you brood

The first step is to monitor yourself to see in what contexts (times of day, places, and situations) you brood and how often you do it. You can do this with a tally counter or a simple tick chart for whenever you ruminate (use the chart below). Becoming more aware of when you are ruminating will enable you to change your behavior.

Interrupting brooding and ruminating

Your goal will be to stop engaging in the content of your brooding and not respond to its incessant demands. As soon as you have noticed yourself brooding or ruminating, refocus attention outwardly on the real world. Choose to do something that you value and which is consistent with the goals that take you closer to long-term reduction in preoccupation with your health.

Self-attacking

Other examples of self-attacking thoughts are:

I'm pathetic	*I'm a failure*	*You're stupid*
You're inferior	*I'm useless*	*You're worthless*
I'm inadequate	*I'm not good enough*	*You're bad*
You're unlovable	*You're worthless*	*You're defective*
I'm fragile	*You're nothing*	

EXERCISE 12.3: BROODING AND WORRYING SELF-MONITORING CHART

Week beginning ____________

Write in your most common brooding and worrying thoughts, and tick the relevant column each time you have that thought, or add the total from your tally counter.

	Mon	Tues	Wed	Thurs	Fri	Sat	Sun
I brood about:							
I brood about:							
I attack myself about:							
I attack myself about:							

Assumptions about self-attacking thoughts

People who are critical of themselves (feeling, for example, that they are ugly, weak, or pathetic) might also have reasons for allowing themselves to be bullied by their minds. It is often helpful to ask yourself, 'What is my greatest fear if I give up criticizing and bullying myself?' Criticism can also act as a warning ('If I don't warn you that you could become ill you might get complacent and forget it'). Sometimes self-criticism can be triggered by a memory or be linked to your identity. Examples of assumptions behind self-criticism in depression are:

If I don't put myself down, then I'll be arrogant.
If I don't get in first with criticism, someone else will.
I attack myself so I can improve myself.
I attack myself so I get the fear I deserve.
If I don't criticize myself, I'll get complacent.

This sort of reasoning is probably an important factor in maintaining long-standing depression and low self-esteem. Take a personal example of one of your own self-attacking thoughts and do a cost-benefit (pros and cons) analysis (see Exercise 5.2 in Chapter 5). Does your attacking really deliver the benefits it promises? Are the costs worth paying? Would being kinder to yourself really leave you worse off? Perhaps you could experiment with a kinder and more compassionate approach to yourself – you could always go back to being attacking if you think it works better!

Compassion and distancing for self-attacking thoughts

As we described in Chapter 4, you can use distancing to minimize the effect of a range of unhelpful thoughts. You can apply the same principles of 'detached observation' to your depressing and self-attacking thoughts as you can to your anxiety-provoking thoughts and images.

It can also be very helpful to build up your levels of compassion towards yourself, since this is incompatible with putting yourself down. Compassion means being warm and understanding about your emotional experience. It means being non-judgmental and sensitive to your own distress and the needs of your mind. It can be helpful to keep in mind Chapter 2, 'How health anxiety develops and is maintained', so that you can see your difficulties in the light of your personal experiences.

MEDICATION FOR DEPRESSION

We describe in Chapter 15 the use of medication which may be helpful in depression.

13

Keeping health anxiety at bay

Once you've make good headway in overcoming your health anxiety, it becomes important to start thinking about how you're going to *stay better* now that you've got better.

You might like to think of your life as a garden, where checking, worrying, safety-seeking and avoidance behaviors are the weeds that have taken root, and probably grown over time. We hope that you've succeeded in pulling up those weeds (sometimes even with the help of a little weed-killer in the form of medication), and planted some desirable plants in the form of new or increased activities and interests, and more helpful ways of coping. Now you need to think about maintaining the garden, which of course means continuing to 'pull up' safety-seeking and avoidance behaviors, worry and the catastrophic misinterpretations that maintain health anxiety. One of the best ways of reducing the chances of weeds growing back is to make sure you pull them up and get the roots out as well, otherwise part of the weed is left in the ground and can grow back again. The parts of health anxiety that are left in your life might be very subtle and something you can live with (such as 'mini' checks, slight avoidance, resisting certain thoughts). To reduce the chances of them growing into something bigger, especially under the 'right' conditions such as times of stress, keep working to get rid of them. Alongside this, you'll need to take ongoing care of your new activities and attitudes to make sure they flourish.

Make a written summary of the gains you have made and how you made them. In the future you may need to recall what you did, so write down a summary of how you have been overcoming your health anxiety using the worksheet below. As well as being extremely useful, this exercise can also help you feel justifiably proud of the changes you've made.

Key techniques checklist

- Have you removed all the safety behaviors (behavioral and mental) and avoidance behaviors that were driven by your health anxiety? If not, what can you do to continue to reduce them? (e.g. resisting the urges to check or seek reassurance and exposure for avoidance).
- Have you managed to reduce your attentional focus on your body and re-trained your attention to focus more readily on the outside world and the here and now.
- Have you focused your mind upon your valued directions in life and begun to live more consistently with these values?

- Have you learned to normalize bodily and mental sensations and reduced your tendency to jump to conclusions about them?
- Can you 'detach' from anxiety-provoking thoughts and allow them to pass through your mind without engaging with them?
- Have you managed to reduce your fears of thoughts, doubts, images and sensations? If not what can you do to reduce these further? (e.g. exposure and behavioral experiments)
- Have you 'filled the gap' left by your health anxiety with interesting, pleasurable, absorbing or satisfying activities? (e.g. new hobbies, work, building relationships, following your valued directions).

What have been the most helpful things you've learned that have helped you overcome your health anxiety?

What have been the most helpful techniques you've applied for benefit in the long term for overcoming your health anxiety?

Keeping psychologically healthy

Try to think of keeping mentally healthy in a similar way to keeping physically healthy. Even if someone has given us a medication to help treat a physical problem, most of us still believe that we need to eat healthily, take appropriate amounts of exercise, and get enough rest to remain physically healthy. Unfortunately though, people all too often seem to think that psychological health is something that can simply be taken for granted, but as anyone who has read this book will now know, this is not so. The following are some ideas for maximizing your psychological health, and therefore reducing the chances of health anxiety returning:

Filling the gap

'Health anxiety loves a vacuum'. Any 'space' left in your life will tend to be filled by health anxiety if you are prone to it. Everyone needs some space in their lives, and many people find it very therapeutic to sit quietly and allow thoughts simply to pass through their minds without engaging with them. However, health anxiety can be a very time-consuming and energy-consuming problem, and research has shown that the extent to which people who are recovering from health anxiety absorb themselves into other activities can have a significant effect on their chances of relapsing.

Many people who have had health anxiety notice that aspects of their lives have been restricted or 'put on hold' because of their fears and rituals. Here are some areas of life to think about. Are there things you would like to do more of? Now is a good time to review your 'valued directions' worksheet from Chapter 3.

Hobbies

What interest have you always wanted to take up but found that fears or lack of time have prevented you? Here is a small range of possibilities (in no particular order) to give you some ideas:

chess	tennis	football
dressmaking	sailing	walking
quizzes	baking	flower arranging

fishing	swimming	gardening
decorating	pottery	painting
jogging	wine tasting	cycling
motorsport	singing	languages
mechanics	squash	basketball
pets	enamelling	antiques
astronomy	jewellery making	cooking
martial Arts	reading	writing
voluntary work	drama	

Work and career

Do you think that your health anxiety has interfered with your seeking work or studying? If you're in work, do you think it has interfered with you advancing your career, or changing careers? This is a common experience for people who have health anxiety. As you get better, start to set goals for how you would like to see your work life develop, and build a realistic and practical action plan for how you will move towards these goals.

Relationships

There is good evidence that a network of social support and a person in your life you can confide in helps to reduce the chances of your suffering from emotional problems in general. Improving your relationships, spending more time with other people and doing things you find enjoyable or worthwhile will also help fill the gap left by your health anxiety as you overcome it. Put simply, your relationships with other people are vitally important in keeping health anxiety at bay.

Improving your relationships

Consider how you would like things to be different in your relationships with other people. Who would you like to make things different with? For example:

- partner or spouse
- children
- relatives
- friends
- colleagues
- neighbours

Many of the changes in your relationships will happen naturally, as you become less preoccupied with your fears, and are more able to focus outside yourself and on the world around you. Good relationships are sustained by time, thought and effort. People recovering from health anxiety often find they have additional problems, though, such as their health anxiety having restricted the amount of time they've spent socializing, their drive for reassurance having shaped their conversations for years. Acting consistently with your personal values on the kind of friend/partner/colleague/son/daughter etc. you'd like to be will help you restore more healthy relationships.

Communicate effectively

It's often said that the lifeblood of any relationship is communication. Keep in mind that we communicate not only by what we say, but also by the way we say things, when and where we say them, and by a variety of non-verbal methods (such as eye contact, body language, spending time, a hug). Here are some tips to improve communication:

- If you have something important to discuss with someone find a mutually good slot with enough time set aside for both of you to talk and listen.
- Use 'I feel' statements like 'I feel disappointed that we couldn't meet up last week' rather than blaming statements like 'You made me so angry'.
- If you want to give feedback to someone on their behavior keep it clear, brief and specific. Remember it's OK to give positive feedback like 'I'd really like to thank you for . . .' as well as saying how you'd like things to be different – 'I'd really appreciate it if you could . . .'.
- If you've given someone some feedback, check how they feel and what they think of what you've said.
- Try to avoid getting stuck in the trap of thinking there is a right or 'true' way of doing something. Value the differences in others, and seek a compromise if appropriate.
- Deal with critical remarks by finding some part of the criticism to agree with, and invite the person to tell you more. This will enable you to evaluate the

criticism effectively and respond in a non-defensive, self-accepting way, such as 'You're right, my health anxiety has made life more difficult for you. I've often worried about the effect it has had on you. What particularly would you like to be different?'

Relapse-prevention – dealing with setbacks

One of the biggest mistakes we see people make is the decision to settle for 'manageable health anxiety'. In our view this is a bit like trying to aim to stay 'a bit pregnant' – sooner or later things are going to develop further! Such a decision leaves you vulnerable to relapse. So in the same way that a bad back sufferer needs to strengthen his back and tummy muscles, people who are recovering from health anxiety need to strengthen their psychological capabilities such as tolerating doubt, non-excessive responsibility, de-catastrophizing, risk-taking, and flexible thinking. They must remain aware of their vulnerability.

Some people may ultimately need to accept a long-term, reduced 'manageable' level of health anxiety, but this will only happen if they continue to work at minimizing it and keeping psychologically healthy. Inevitably you will have setbacks form time to time. Note there is an important distinction to be made between a relapse and a setback. A relapse means a 'back to the beginning' slip in your health anxiety, whereas a setback is a slip backward on the road to recovery. The good news is that neither is a hopeless situation, but by dealing effectively with setbacks you can dramatically reduce the chances of a relapse.

Setbacks are a normal part of recovery

The 'two steps forward, one step back' experience is common in many endeavours, and overcoming health anxiety is no different. Don't panic if you slip back, but do try to see if you can learn anything about why you slipped backwards. A few examples are:

- Encountering a previously avoided trigger, which can now become part of your exposure hierarchy;
- Allowing yourself 'small amounts of ritual', such as a 'quick check', which then escalates, serving as a reminder of how firmly you need to resist rituals;
- Discovering that you've been relying on certain conditions to do exposure and response prevention (e.g. after discussing it with someone) and then finding it difficult to manage without these conditions (in this case you need to redesign your exposures to be more independent);
- Having become complacent about exposure and response prevention without having done sufficient work to remove the fear, allowing your fear to grow.

Whilst setbacks are disappointing, you can make the most of them if you use them as an opportunity to learn about the strengths and weaknesses of your recovery, and then make a plan that builds on your strengths as well as minimizing your weaknesses. Try to make a plan on how to deal with setbacks by considering the following.

1 What events or situations might trigger a setback?

How could you plan to tackle these events or situations to minimize their impact? What you could do to practise coping with them?

2 Act sooner rather than later

To reduce the chances of a setback becoming more serious it's helpful to take action to tackle it as early as you can. What might be early warning signs that your health anxiety is beginning to creep back in?

3 In order for you to maintain your gains what are the main things you need to work at?

14

Helping someone overcome health anxiety

This chapter is primarily written for family members or friends of people with health anxiety. It will be of most help if the person who suffers from health anxiety has read through this book, and is actively seeking to overcome his or her problem. If this is the case, the most helpful thing you, as a helper, can do is become an ally for the individual in overcoming their health anxiety, if he or she wishes you to.

To recover from health anxiety lots of the right kind of hard work and brain-training is needed. However, the fact remains that it's not how much you (the therapist, partner, relative, friend, doctor, helper, etc.) want the person with health anxiety to change that counts, but rather that the person with health anxiety has to be in the driving seat. Even where professional therapy is concerned, you can only take the horse to water – you cannot make it drink. The key is to encourage the person with health anxiety to 'try out' treating their problem 'as if' it's a problem of worrying about their health to see how it works out (see Chapter 2). You can say that you are prepared to support them if they are prepared to fully commit themselves and do the exercises consistently for at least three months. If the approach doesn't work then they can always go back to seeing more doctors and having further tests.

In cognitive behavioral therapy (CBT), the person who acts as an ally in this way is sometimes called a 'co-therapist'. Such allies can be of enormous value and can help in numerous ways. If you decide to be an ally or co-therapist for a person with health anxiety, it will make sense for both of you to work through this book, and review it together as you progress. However, be aware that you, the co-therapist, may come to feel that the person you are trying to help is over-involved with monitoring their homework or progress. If this happens, both of you will need to re-negotiate your degree of involvement.

General guidelines for relatives

Know your enemy!

If you are a relative or a friend of someone with health anxiety, and especially if you are partner of someone with health anxiety, get to know as much as you can about the condition (for example, by reading books like this one), the common behaviors and the treatments available. It's worth emphasizing three key points:

- However odd the behaviors may seem, they are just part of health anxiety. Health anxiety is not a sign of madness – it's simply a disorder, of the kind that can affect many people at some stage in their lives.

The behavior of someone with health anxiety is neither 'bad' nor done to annoy you.

- If you have a relative or partner with health anxiety, it's still important to set consistent boundaries with behaviors that are unrelated to health anxiety, and to problem-solve health anxiety behavior where it impinges on your family life (for example, the length of time the person spends researching information on the Internet).
- Health anxiety is not something that can be easily stopped. It will take time, commitment, and the right guidance to improve everyone's quality of life. Each person needs to overcome his or her problems at an individual pace, even though this may be a lengthy process. Avoid comparing your relative or friend to other individuals with a mental health problem or indeed without it.

Avoid the blame game

No one should be blamed for health anxiety – it's not the fault of the person who has it, and nor is it the fault of a relative. If you are a parent there is no need to feel guilty for 'causing' health anxiety, even if there is a possible genetic link. If you start blaming your genes then you can go all the way back to Adam and Eve!

Encourage your relative to seek help

Encourage your relative with health anxiety to try out the principles explained in this book, and to seek professional help with therapy or medication if they need it. Support them in either or both routes, and do everything you can to help them change. This means:

- helping them to understand and define their problems clearly
- if they want you to, being an ally as described above
- encouraging them to persist with their treatment
- and praising any improvement, however small.

Don't participate in health anxiety

Families should not try to adapt their ways of doing things to accommodate a relative's worries. Don't put family life on hold. Accept that health anxiety may complicate family life, but get on with it anyway, and encourage your relative to maintain as normal a lifestyle as possible:

- Don't collaborate in trying to find 'magic solutions', such as cutting details about health scans out of the paper or offering to pay private doctors appointments or provide a loan.
- Don't provide reassurance. This is of course easier said than done, but we discuss alternatives below.

- Don't take on the responsibilities of the person with health anxiety (unless of course you are a parent of a child).
- Don't make excuses for them (for their being late for work or for an appointment, for example).
- If necessary, compromise in the short term in the way we have described, but draw the line when new avoidance behaviors and safety behaviors start.

If you have been participating in your relative's health anxiety up to now, start to find ways of changing this:

- If the person is in therapy, ask your relative if you can see the therapist with him or her and discuss a program of reducing your involvement in your relative's health anxiety.
- If the person is not in therapy, try to negotiate a program of gradual withdrawal from the person's reassurance-seeking and checking safety and avoidance behavior before you implement it.
- Make sure that you communicate that you are changing your involvement in order to help rather than punish.
- Practise saying 'No' or 'No, thank you' to requests for reassurance or checking.
- Help your relative to see the downside of you participating in avoidance and safety behaviors and

the effect on your relationship. Highlight how long the effect of the reassurance lasts for and what the effect is on their doubts. In other words, try not to respond to the content of their worries but focus them more on the questioning the process of what they are doing. (For example, use questions that help your relative reflect on the effect of giving reassurance on your relationship and on their health anxiety).

Anticipate how you will deal with your relative becoming stressed or irritated by your new way of responding and have a plan that you can both agree upon if he or she becomes aggressive or angry. You may have to be very persistent until requests for reassurance stop happening, because if you respond just once, it immediately becomes more likely that they will involve you again.

Remember:

- Individuals with health anxiety will not come to any harm as a result of anxiety, though they may be distressed in the short term.
- Accommodating rituals and avoidance means that you are helping to fuel health anxiety in the long term – and you are not taking care of yourself. It may feel as if you're protecting yourself from stress and helping someone with health anxiety, but the effect can be the opposite.

- What is good for the family is good for the person with health anxiety, and this can only occur when no one else engages in the health anxiety. A family that is pulling together can provide better support for your relative with health anxiety. Its members can also better support each other and solve problems more efficiently.

Be a coach and cheerleader

You and your relative both need to see health anxiety, not the individual experiencing it, as your shared enemy. Approach the problem as a team, working together. As your relative improves, see yourself as a coach shouting encouragement from the sidelines, or cheerleading, as you become less involved. Enthusiasm, understanding and general support really are the best help you can provide.

Look after your own needs

You need to follow your own interests and have your own sources of support. At times you may need time out (or respite care). When this happens, tell your relative that you need a break but that you have not given up on them, and try to get others to help in your place.

Feelings such as guilt, sadness and anger are normal in those caring for a relative with any long-term disability.

- Try not to engage in self-pitying thoughts such as 'Why me?' or 'Poor me, I don't deserve to have health anxiety in the family.' These will only make you feel worse and feed another vicious circle.
- Try to detach yourself emotionally from your relative's health anxiety and take it less personally.
- If you're not coping emotionally or it is affecting other areas of your life, seek help. There may be a local caregivers' group or, even better, a group for caregivers of individuals with health anxiety. Alternatively, see your family doctor for a referral or go directly to a therapist.

De-catastrophize anxiety and discomfort

We've met many family members who seem to share the view of people with health anxiety that any anxiety or discomfort should be avoided, and have even been critical of CBT because it requires a tolerance of discomfort. In some cases this is entirely understandable, given the profound distress that the individual with health anxiety, whom they care about, experiences as they wrestle with a doubt or intrusive thoughts.

But some families share 'rules' about emotions that can be *unhelpful* in overcoming health anxiety. For example, they believe that:

- Emotions are a sign of weakness and should be controlled.
- If something upsets you, don't think about it.
- Being upset is terrible, and it's important to do something to make yourself feel better as soon as possible.
- If something bothers you, you should do something to take your mind off it.
- You should be careful about showing that you feel upset to other people, in case they use it against you.
- If you get too upset it could make you ill, so it's best to avoid intense emotions.

These rules are unhelpful since they interfere with a person's ability to recover from health anxiety. They are sometimes explicitly taught; at other times they are taught by the way a family or person within that family behaves.

If you think you or your family shares any rules like these, which might make experiencing emotions even harder, try to communicate to the person with health anxiety the message that you are confident that feeling short-term distress is a sensible and helpful thing when overcoming health anxiety.

Be prepared for setbacks

It's likely that on some days your relative will be better able to deal with symptoms than on others. It will be harder for both of you at certain times – for example, when either of you is feeling tired or stressed by other problems. Setbacks are to be expected, and to a certain extent can be planned for. Taking time out can be helpful at these points.

Each person with health anxiety will need to overcome their problems at their own pace, even though this may be a lengthy process. It's entirely normal to experience setbacks along the road to recovery. Don't lose heart. You can help by staying optimistic and encouraging the person to keep trying. You probably won't see the hundred times that health anxiety doesn't get in the way, but you are bound to notice the time that it does!

Keep a sense of humour

People with health anxiety are often aware of the humorous aspects of their worries. However, it is very important that friends and relatives resist any temptation to mock the person with health anxiety for their symptoms because this may cause additional stress, shame and embarrassment.

Keep communicating

Make sure that you keep talking both with your relative who has health anxiety and with everyone else in your family.

- Remember that you may need help and support yourself.

- Make sure that you continue to do things you enjoy and have people to talk to about your own feelings and concerns.
- Eventually, you may decide that, for the sake of your own mental health, you can't carry on caring for your relative with health anxiety. In that case you'll need to communicate as a family and get help from the local services.

What if a relative plays down the problem?

If your relative insists that health anxiety is having hardly any effect on their life, there are various things you can do to encourage them to face up to the problem and seek help. Try to find out:

- what their real feelings are about having such a problem (shame, for example, can make people very reluctant to acknowledge it; see Chapter 3 in this book)
- what they fear
- and/or what doubts they have about therapy or change.

Ensure that as a family, or if possible as a wider group, including friends, you take a consistent approach, and that nobody is accommodating the health anxiety. Agree upon your message, and if necessary talk to the individual both within the family (or wider) group and with a mental health professional.

One person in the group might draw up, along with the relative with health anxiety, a list of costs (or disadvantages) and benefits (advantages) of:

a) staying the way they are, or
b) engaging in a program of therapy.

A blank copy of the cost-benefit analysis form can be found on page 106. Each of the costs and benefits may be divided into those for the 'self' and those for 'others'. Even if your relative sees few disadvantages in staying in the same condition, you can emphasize the costs of health anxiety to others in the family and the benefits to him- or herself in the long term. Continue to emphasize that you will still provide support and help during therapy. If your relative finally agrees to seek help, discuss the timeframe within which this can be done, and the process it will involve.

What if a relative refuses to seek help?

If your relative has very severe health anxiety, continues to refuse help and you decide that you cannot go on any longer with things the way they are, you will need to explore your own options, such as finding your relative independent living arrangements by getting help from your local mental health services.

Local mental health services do not always respond

positively to requests for help with these cases. The main priority for a psychiatrist in public health services is patients with 'severe mental illness', especially those who may be suicidal or a danger to the community. UK and US mental health law allows a patient to be detained in hospital against their will in certain circumstances; but in the absence of a risk to themselves or self-neglect, patients with health anxiety are unlikely to be admitted to a hospital and would, in any case, be unlikely to benefit much from admission to the average acute psychiatric ward. Short-term in-patient care in a national specialist unit where the staff are used to dealing with health anxiety patients and where regular CBT is available, is more likely to be helpful. In others a trial of medication may be given against a person's will, which can be helpful to some people, especially those who have lost touch with reality or are severely depressed.

It must be emphasized, though, that CBT is powerless without the cooperation of a person with health anxiety. It is both unethical and counter-productive to forcibly expose someone to feared situations or activities. Therapists may encourage and challenge a patient, but would never force exposure or spring something on their patient unannounced. Nor should you ever do this to a relative with health anxiety. A program of CBT has to be followed voluntarily, and the motivation has to come from the patient, if it is to be ethical and effective.

Remember: Recovery from health anxiety is a process

When your relative or friend is recovering, you may expect everything to go back to how it used to be. Yet this may not be how it happens at all, and the family may need to go through various stages of adjustment. This is normal. Each person will adjust and recover at a different rate. You may want to see health anxiety as something that is 'over' or 'finished', but remember that setbacks are part of the process.

In summary, health anxiety can have a profound effect on the person with health anxiety and on the person or people who looks after them. However, though the situation may sometimes be difficult, it is never hopeless, and there is a lot that you can do as a team to help each other.

15

A guide to medication for health anxiety

By discussing the potential benefits and disadvantages of taking medication for health anxiety, this chapter aims to help you make an informed choice about whether or not you wish to pursue this course of action. The discussion may also be relevant for someone who is severely depressed. However if, after reading this chapter, you have doubts and questions about medication, discuss it with your doctor rather than just ignoring a prescription or stopping your medication.

If you have been recommended medication and decide to take it, it is also important that you take it in the correct dose and frequency. The possible side effects and what you can do to minimize them are also discussed in this chapter. In addition, we provide advice on how to come off anti-depressant medication. Being well informed is vital because for some people prescribed medication will not be dispensed at the pharmacy, and others may take it inappropriately (for example, at a lower dose than recommended or not daily) or not at all.

Medication that may be suggested

- as an alternative to cognitive behavior therapy (CBT)
- in addition to CBT if you have severe symptoms of health anxiety
- if you have health anxiety and are also significantly depressed.

You may find it difficult to be offered CBT because of long waiting lists or other restrictions in public medicine and insurance cover. As a result, you may be offered medication before you receive CBT. More research is needed on how best to optimize combined treatments in health anxiety. We think that CBT and medication are as effective as one another for most people with health anxiety, though we don't yet have published research evidence to support this. It is certainly very important that individuals have a choice – unfortunately CBT may be more costly to provide than drug therapy in the short term. Yet, in the long term, psychological treatments are usually more cost-effective, as the cost of the drug continues for several months and if medication is used alone and it is stopped there is a higher risk of relapse as compared with an effective psychological therapy.

Some individuals may do better on a combination of CBT and medication than either treatment alone. This is usually recommended when you fail to respond adequately to CBT or if your health anxiety is severe. The problem is that no one can predict with any certainty as to who will respond best to which treatment.

Isn't taking medication a sign of weakness?

Taking medication is not a sign of weakness or failure. You probably wouldn't think this a possibility if you had heart disease or cancer. Your relatives and friends are more likely to think of your behavior as weak if you don't take medication and find it difficult to understand why you don't do everything you can to get better. If some of them do criticize you, they probably don't understand what you are experiencing and their opinion is not worth considering. Mental disorder is no different from other medical problems in this respect, and taking medication is a practical approach.

How quickly does medication work?

Even if medication is of benefit, it will not work right away. Most people notice some improvement in their symptoms after about four to six weeks, while maximum benefit should occur within four months. It is important to continue to take your medication at the highest dose you can tolerate (as prescribed by your doctor) for this period before judging how effective it has been.

How long will I need to take medication for?

Never stop taking medication without discussing it with your doctor first, and always ensure that you have another prescription ready before you run out of drugs. This is because if you do not take medication regularly or stop it suddenly (for example, if you forget to take it on holiday), you may be at risk of experiencing withdrawal symptoms. This is discussed in detail at the end of the chapter.

Once you have recovered from health anxiety or depression and stop taking medication, you may find you relapse if you have had no other therapy. The risk of relapse will partly depend on the natural pattern of your health anxiety without treatment. For example, for a first episode of health anxiety the chance of recurrence is less if you continue to take an antidepressant for up to a year after you have recovered. If you have a second episode of health anxiety, then your chances of relapse are lower if you keep taking an antidepressant for a couple of years after you have got better. If you are someone whose health anxiety keeps recurring, then the risk of relapse is much higher and you may be advised to remain on the medication for at least five years. Certain people may need to be on medication for many years to reduce the risk of relapse.

For many, the risk of relapse is minimized by combining medication with CBT. If you are planning to stop medication, ensure you do so after discussion with your doctor and within an agreed time frame. Be aware that your depressive symptoms may start to return within a few weeks or months, so don't plan to stop before predictable major stresses and life events.

SSRIs

The first choice of medication for most people with health anxiety or depression is a class of antidepressants called Selective Serotonergic Reuptake Inhibitors (or SSRIs for short; see Table 15.1). 'Serotonergic' means that the drugs act on serotonin nerve endings in the brain. 'Selective' refers to the fact that they act on serotonin nerve endings rather than others such as noradrenaline or histamine nerve endings. 'Reuptake Inhibitor' refers to the way the drug acts: it helps to increase the concentration of serotonin in the nerve cells. This in turn helps to increase the messages passing along certain pathways in the brain and so to reduce anxiety.

For health anxiety, an SSRI may reduce your preoccupation and distress with health. In health anxiety, a part of your nervous system may have an excessive load on it as your mind tries to make things better. SSRIs enhance this normal activity of the brain and improve its ability to dampen anxiety and reduce your preoccupation. SSRIs are also used for panic attacks, obsessive compulsive disorder and depression; they are not used specifically for health anxiety. A family doctor may prescribe the drug or may refer you to a psychiatrist who can discuss any issues you may have in detail.

Which SSRI might be prescribed?

In general, all SSRIs are likely to be equally effective for health anxiety or depression, but people respond differently to different drugs. However, your doctor will help you choose the most appropriate SSRI for you given your circumstances and medical history. For example, citalopram or escitalopram are usually well tolerated and are a good choice if you are on other drugs at the same time. Citalopram is a mixture of two molecules, which are identical except that they are mirror images of each other. Escitalopram is the molecule that has the serotonin action and is available without a redundant molecule, which had no serotonin action. The result is the same whichever of the two you take, but escitalopram may have slightly fewer side effects.

Fluoxetine takes longer to be metabolized by the body, so if you forget a dose one day, you can get away with it because it does not vanish from the blood when you stop taking it. It is also now the cheapest of the SSRIs and the easiest to stop taking. However, some people find fluoxetine slightly more likely to increase anxiety when they first start taking the drug. Some SSRIs such as paroxetine may be more difficult to withdraw from (see the section 'Stopping taking antidepressant medication' on page 265).

If you or someone in your family did well or poorly with a medication in the past, this may influence what your doctor prescribes for you. If you have medical problems (for example, problems sleeping) or are taking another medication, these factors may also influence your doctor's choice, since he or she will pay particular attention to possible side effects and drug interactions, in order to minimize them. Make sure you tell your doctor if you:

- are pregnant or plan to get pregnant or are breast-feeding
- have any other medical conditions are taking any other medication or herbal drugs like St John's Wort.

Can I drink alcohol with an SSRI?

In general, you can drink alcohol as long as you do so in moderation and do not binge-drink. However, people's reactions to alcohol do vary when taking medication and some people can become more aggressive or sedated. See how you respond to one drink initially.

Fluvoxamine and sertraline may not mix very well with alcohol so be aware that this mix may impair your judgement; also, when you are on one of these, you should not drive or operate machinery. Excessive alcohol can also be a factor in depression and will interfere in your recovery. Compared with the older antidepressants, SSRIs are generally safe. An overdose will not generally harm you.

What dose of an SSRI should I be prescribed?

The normal starting dose and suitable target doses of different SSRIs are listed in Table 15.1. When progress is slow, there is some evidence that you may need to increase the dose. If you experience significant side effects, you can always start on a lower dose after discussion with your doctor. You can then build the dose up slowly under the guidance of your doctor. Tablets should be swallowed with some water while sitting or standing. This is to make sure that they do not stick in your throat. If you miss a dose, take it as soon as you remember it. However, if it is almost time for the next dose, skip the missed dose and continue your regular dose. Do not take a double dose to make up for a missed one.

Table 15.1 SSRI antidepressants

Chemical name	Common trade names	Usual starting dose	Usual maximum dose	Liquid Preparation
Citalopram	Cipramil, Celexa	20mg	50mg	Yes (20mg=5ml)
Escitalopram	Cipralex, Lexapro	10mg	20mg	Yes (5mg=5ml)
Fluoxetine	Prozac	20mg	60mg	Yes (20mg=5ml)
Fluvoxamine	Faverin, Luvox	50mg	200mg	No
Paroxetine	Seroxat, Paxil	20mg	60mg	Yes (10mg=5ml)
Sertraline	Lustral, Zoloft	50mg	200mg	Yes (100mg=5ml)

Can vegans have SSRIs?

Citalopram elixir, fluoxetine elixir, clomipramine elixir, sertraline tablets and paroxetine tablets or liquid do not contain any animal products.

What about reports of SSRIs causing suicide?

There is some evidence that a few antidepressants can cause a slight increase in suicidal ideas (not acts) in young people. For young people, the increased risk of suicidal ideas is extremely small. Provided that you monitor such feelings, talk about them openly with your doctor and relatives, and are seen regularly, this is something that can be managed. The thoughts of suicide will then decrease as your depression lifts.

Antidepressant medication for children and adolescents

Antidepressant medication for children with health anxiety or depression has not been well studied to date, and so CBT is usually recommended as the first line of treatment. This is because scientists don't yet know the long-term effects of antidepressants on the immature brain of a child and also because antidepressants are often ineffective in young people or may be associated with a slight increase in suicidal ideas (see above). Equally, this needs to be judged against the risk of a young person with severe depression not using medication or not responding to CBT (or refuses it). If he or she is continuing to experience severe depression, this may have a major adverse impact on both development and education. In such cases, an antidepressant is recommended. Only fluoxetine has been shown in controlled trials to have a favourable balance of risks and benefits for the treatment of depression in the under-18s, and this is the SSRI that might be recommended. The dose should usually start at a half the adult dose (10mg) and may be increased gradually. A psychiatrist should supervise the use of an antidepressant for a child or adolescent and monitor his or her mental state closely (for example, weekly for the first four weeks). An SSRI should be offered in combination with an evidence-based psychological treatment. If treatment with fluoxetine is unsuccessful or is not tolerated because of side effects, consideration should be given to the use of another antidepressant. In this case, sertraline or citalopram might be second-line treatments. Guidelines recommend that venlafaxine (Efexor) and paroxetine

(Seroxat, Paxil) and clomipramine antidepressants should not be used for the treatment of depression in children and young people. The side effects listed below occur in children as they do in adults. In addition, children may become over-excited, irritable or 'silly'; if these features become severe there may be reason to stop the medication.

What side effects occur with SSRIs?

Some people experience side effects with SSRIs, but those who do normally find them to be minor irritations which usually decrease after a few weeks. Most people find that they are not usually a problem in the long term. They will not alter your personality or turn you into a zombie, and will cease when you stop taking the drug. The worst side effects usually occur in the first few days or weeks after commencing the drug. This is the time when you are most likely to stop taking the drug because you have not experienced any improvement in the symptoms of your depression. (This is because it takes four to six weeks for the full benefits of the medication to become clear.) There is one side effect that does not tend to improve over time: sexual difficulties. However, side effects that persist, including those of a sexual nature, will decrease when you stop taking the medication.

You are more likely to experience side effects if you are on a large dose or if your dose has been rapidly increased. If you are unable to tolerate the medication, you can try reducing the dose and then increasing it to the previous level more slowly. For example, if you find that you are feeling nauseous after a few days of taking

20mg of fluoxetine or paroxetine, you can reduce the dose to 10mg for a week or two and then increase it to 20mg again when your body has become more accustomed to the drug. This can also be done if it is a liquid, increasing the dose very slowly. Another alternative is to switch to a different SSRI altogether.

The possible side effects of SSRIs and how to deal with them are given below. The list looks rather daunting but remember that the symptoms occur in a minority of people. They stop if you discontinue the drug under guidance from your doctor. Alternatively, your doctor may discuss with you how to manage them better. Careful monitoring of your health anxiety and possible side effects is the key to all treatments – keep track of how you feel with a standard measure such as the Health Anxiety Inventory in Chapter 3 and use it like a temperature chart on a weekly basis. If your mood is not improving, and especially if you are you are becoming more suicidal, discuss the issue with your therapist or psychiatrist and consider whether you need to change tack. Always discuss reducing or increasing any prescribed dosage with your doctor or psychiatrist.

Nausea

Nausea (feeling sick) is the most common but temporary side effect of an SSRI and affects about 25 per cent of patients taking an SSRI compared with about 10 per cent of those on a placebo. Citalopram and fluvoxamine are slightly more likely than the other SSRIs to cause nausea. The feeling can be minimized by taking the drug after food. Alternatively, halve the dose for a couple of weeks and then increase it slowly back to the normal dose. If the nausea still persists, an antinausea drug (for example, metoclobemide) may help.

Diarrhoea or constipation

SSRIs can cause diarrhoea in up to 15 per cent of patients compared with about 5 per cent who take a placebo. Diarrhoea can be minimized by drinking plenty of apple juice (which contains pectin) or the use of the drug bismuth subsalicylate (Kaopectate). Constipation occurs in 5 per cent of patients taking an SSRI. Diarrhoea or constipation may be improved by taking bulking agents such as Fybogel or psyllium seed husk and eating plenty of bran and roughage. For both diarrhoea and constipation, you should drink at least 2 litres of water a day.

Headache

Up to 20 per cent of patients taking an SSRI find they develop headaches. Headache is a common symptom of tension and occurs in about 15 per cent of patients taking a placebo. Symptoms of headache can usually be helped by simple painkillers such as paracetamol and should decrease after a few weeks of taking an SSRI.

Excessive sweating

Excessive sweating occurs in about 10 per cent of patients taking an SSRI compared with 5 per cent of those taking a placebo. There is no easy solution to this problem, although it should decrease over time.

Dry mouth

Dry mouth affects about 10 per cent of patients taking an SSRI compared with 5 per cent of those taking a placebo. Sucking on sugarless gum or sugar-free boiled sweets may stimulate production of saliva, or you could try a spray that can be bought over the counter that provides artificial saliva. Again, the symptoms usually decrease over time.

Tremor

Shakiness or tremor occurs in about 10 per cent of patients taking an SSRI and 3 per cent of those on a placebo. A betablocker (for example, propranolol) may be prescribed to help reduce tremor if it is severe.

Sedation or insomnia

Between 10 and 20 per cent of patients on SSRIs feel sedated and between 5 and 15 per cent cannot sleep. For some SSRIs, the problem can sometimes be resolved by changing the time of day you take your medication (take it at night, for example, if it makes you drowsy), temporarily reducing the dose, or taking a different SSRI altogether. Fluoxetine may be activating and should normally be taken in the mornings. Sertraline is less likely to cause sedation. Fluvoxamine and trazodone are more likely to cause sedation and are best prescribed at night. If sedation is a problem, do not drive or use machinery.

Sexual problems

Sexual side effects of SSRIs can take the form of delayed ejaculation in men and an inability to reach an orgasm in women. They can also occasionally cause both men and women to lose libido, although this is complicated to assess in the presence of depression. (However, there is one case report of an SSRI causing orgasms with yawning!)

Some atypical serotonergic antidepressants do not cause delayed ejaculation, but their benefit in health anxiety is not known. Trazodone is one example, which very rarely in men can cause 'priapism', which is a persistent and painful erection and which should be treated as an emergency at a casualty department. Nefazadone was similar to trazodone but did not cause delayed ejaculation or erectile problems; unfortunately, it was withdrawn by the manufacturers for commercial reasons and is now only available on a named-patient basis. Another antidepressant to consider if sexual dysfunction is a problem is reboxetine or lofepramine, which both act on the noradrenergic nervous system. However, they are likely to be less effective for health anxiety.

In the case of SSRIs generally, if you are on a relatively high dose the problem of sexual side effects can sometimes be solved by lowering the dose or taking a drug holiday and missing a dose on the day of sexual activity. This needs to be done with caution though, as you may experience some withdrawal symptoms (see below). Taking a drug holiday is usually safe with fluoxetine, which remains in body for up to five weeks after stopping taking it.

Another possible solution is ginkgo biloba. This is a herbal extract of the maidenhead hair tree and is sometimes used to enhance memory, particularly in the elderly. It can be purchased in healthfood shops. Ginkgo biloba has been used to treat sexual problems caused by antidepressant drugs in a series of fourteen patients. They had a variety of difficulties, including erectile problems, delayed ejaculation, loss of libido and an inability to reach orgasm. The patients took a daily dose of 240mg for six weeks. The only side effect was gastric irritation (reported by two patients). Overall, the group reported improvements. Two out of the fourteen patients reported no improvements and two reported that sexual functioning was completely restored. This study needs to be done as a controlled trial, but in the meantime gingko biloba may be worth trying as a natural supplement. It would also be sensible to discuss this with your doctor.

There are also reports concerning the use of Viagra or Cialis for men and women taking SSRIs. Viagra has been reported as successful in reversing the sexual side effects of SSRIs. Again, this needs to be researched carefully. If you wish to take Viagra, try a dose of 50mg one hour before sexual activity, having first discussed it with your doctor. If this does not improve things or gives only a partial response, you could try increasing it to 100mg. Some patients with heart conditions will not be able to take the drug. Cialis has a possible advantage of a longer lasting effect. The possible side effects of Viagra and Cialis include headache, flushing and dizziness. Do not buy such drugs from the Internet as you have no guarantee of quality and they could just be dummy pills or worse.

Loss of appetite

Symptoms of loss of appetite and weight loss occur in between 5 and 10 per cent of patients taking SSRIs (especially with fluoxetine). Reducing the dose can halt this effect, though the symptoms usually fade away over time anyway. Some SSRIs can sometimes cause slight weight gain in the long term and you may need to adjust your diet and exercise program. Depression and inactivity will also contribute to weight gain.

Nervousness or agitation

Some people feel more anxious or 'wired' or more impulsive when starting an SSRI. This may be more common with fluoxetine, which may then cause agitation or insomnia if taken too late in the day. Sertraline may be less likely to cause anxiety. It is always difficult to tell whether anxiety is associated with the depression and what is caused by the drug. If it is caused by the drug, the problem may be solved by a) trying a lower dose or b) switching to a different SSRI. The feeling of increased anxiety is usually temporary and will subside over time. Feelings of increased agitation in some SSRIs may rarely be associated with an increase in ideas of violence or suicide. This is more likely to occur in a young person. If this happens, seek urgent medical advice. The feelings will subside on gradual withdrawal of the medication and you may need a different therapy or type of antidepressant.

Rashes

Rashes are rare, but if you do get one, you will probably need to speak to your doctor and stop taking your medication. This is more likely to occur with fluoxetine.

Mania

Antidepressants can very occasionally induce mania, especially in a person prone to bipolar disorder. You may be overactive, disinhibited, full of energy, irritable and able to go without any sleep. This condition can involve dangerous or risky behaviors. You should seek medical attention quickly. You may be advised to discontinue the medication.

Side effects of SSRIs

Whenever side effects are a problem, always discuss them with your doctor. The doctor is likely to advise you to:

- either reduce the dose
- or try a different SSRI
- or add another medication to counteract side effects such as insomnia or sexual problems
- or perhaps wait and see, as many of the side effects tend to improve over time.

All SSRIs are equally effective overall, but one person may get a better response from one than another or your doctor may wish to try you on another or a different class of antidepressant according to how well your mood improves or how troublesome your side effects are.

Tricyclics

Tricyclics are an older class of antidepressants: they were first developed for the treatment of depression and obsessive compulsive disorder in the 1960s. The name 'tricyclic' is used to describe the structure of the chemical which was first synthesized.

Tricyclics lost favour in relation to SSRIs because they have more side effects. Clomipramine (trade name Anafranil) is a tricylic that is used for treating health anxiety because compared to other tricyclics it is a potent serotonin reuptake inhibitor. It can also be used for depression. It is normally started with a low dosage (for example, 75mg at night) and gradually increased to a maximum that you can tolerate. The minimum dose required for an effect is usually 125mg. Higher doses are sometimes used up to 300mg a day, although the usual dose is up to 225mg. Higher doses tend to increase the frequency of side effects. Most of the side effects are related to the dose and tend to reduce over time, but some may persist. They will cease if the drug is discontinued. Clomipramine is more often prescribed at night so that the sedative side effects have worn off by the morning. Some people metabolize a tricyclic very quickly and so even when they are taking a high dose they may have a relatively low level of the drug in the bloodstream. If necessary, the level of a tricyclic and its metabolite can be checked by a blood test to determine if it is safe to increase the dose to a higher level. Alternatively, you may be given a genetic test to see if you are someone who metabolizes such drugs faster than others.

Common side-effects of clomipramine

Dry mouth: At least two-thirds of patients taking clomipramine experience a dry mouth. You get a dry mouth when you produce less saliva than normal. Sucking on sugarless gum may stimulate production of saliva or you could try a spray that can be bought over the counter that provides artificial saliva. Good mouth hygiene is important, as is a regular visit to your dentist.

Dizziness: Dizziness on standing up is a common side effect for about 25 per cent of patients taking clomipramine. You can minimize dizziness by rising slowly or sitting on the side of the bed or chair and squeezing the muscles in your calf as you stand up.

Tremor: About 15 per cent of patients taking clomipramine develop shakiness or a tremor in their arms. There are no simple remedies for tremor although another drug (a betablocker, such as propranolol) may reduce a tremor if it is severe.

Weight gain: Weight gain can be a problem with clomipramine and you should therefore be especially careful to eat healthily when taking this drug.

Constipation: You have a one in four chance of becoming constipated if you take a clomipramine. A diet full of roughage from vegetables or bran and prunes or a bulking agent such as Fybogel or psyllium husks will help. Always remember to drink plenty of water. Laxatives that stimulate the bowel should not be used except occasionally.

Drowsiness or fatigue: Clomipramine can cause drowsiness which can be minimized by taking the dosage at night. Some people may still experience a hangover in the morning: if this happens with you, spread the dose over the day.

Blurred vision, headache: Clomipramine can also cause blurring of vision or a headache. There is no good solution to this apart from switching to a different antidepressant.

Sexual problems: Clomipramine can be a reason for delayed ejaculation or, less commonly, impotence in men. It can also cause women difficulties in reaching orgasm. For suggested solutions see under side effects of SSRIs.

Increased sweating: People taking clomipramine may complain that they sweat more or that their hot flushes have increased. There is no easy solution to this, but it should improve over time.

Epileptic fit: There is a small risk (for about 0.5 per cent of individuals taking clomipramine) of having an epileptic fit. In this case, the drug will need to be discontinued or the dose significantly reduced. The majority of fits, however, occur in patients taking above 250mg of clomipramine.

Urinary problems: Occasionally, clomipramine can cause urinary retention or hesitancy in the elderly, in which case the drug will need to be discontinued.

Heart problems: Individuals with pre-existing heart disease treated with a clomipramine should have an ECG (electrocardiogram) before beginning treatment and at regular intervals during treatment since it can cause some individuals to develop an irregular heartbeat.

There are a few other classes of antidepressants (other than SSRIs and a tricyclic) which are sometimes used in health anxiety.

Stopping taking antidepressant medication

If you are already taking antidepressant medication, then don't stop or change the dose on your own initiative. It's best to reduce such medication slowly because you may experience withdrawal symptoms from the antidepressant. Whether or not this is the case with you is unpredictable – many people do not have any or only minor withdrawal symptoms; a small minority have marked or severe symptoms that require careful reduction of their medication. Note that some doctors may refer to withdrawal symptoms as 'discontinuation', which is partly a euphemism to avoid the association with an addiction or dependence. However, it is now generally recognized that, for a few people, it is a type of addiction in that the stopping of the drug may cause withdrawal symptoms and craving. The body finds it difficult to adapt if a drug is removed suddenly and it is sensible therefore to taper the dose gradually over several weeks. Withdrawal symptoms can be minimized or prevented if you are pre-warned and manage the situation. Always discuss your wishes with your doctor and plan things together. Do not be afraid to ask for a second opinion where necessary.

The speed at which the discontinuation of a drug causes withdrawal symptoms is related to how fast the drug is metabolized and gets out of your system. Fluoxetine is the least likely of all SSRIs to cause withdrawal symptoms. This is because it breaks down very slowly and is in your body for up to five weeks after your last dose. If it does cause withdrawal symptoms, they tend to come on within two or three weeks of stopping it. The worst drugs linked to withdrawal symptoms are venlafaxine (Efexor) and paroxetine (Seroxat, Paxil), which can cause symptoms on the same day you miss a dose. Sertraline (Zoloft) commonly causes withdrawal symptoms within two to three days.

Possible physical withdrawal symptoms can include the following.

- flu-like symptoms (aches, fever, sweats, chills, muscle cramps)
- gastroenteritis-like symptoms (nausea, vomit, diarrhoea, abdominal pain or cramps)
- dizziness, spinning, feeling hung over, feeling unsteady
- headache, tremor
- sensory abnormalities (numbness, sensations that feel like electric shocks, abnormal visual sensations or smells, tinnitus).

The second group of symptoms that can occur are predominantly psychological.

- depression (crying, deteriorating mood, fatigue, poor concentration, loss of appetite, suicidal thoughts/attempts)
- anxiety-like symptoms (anxious, nervous, panicky)
- a preoccupation and distress with one's appearance
- irritability (agitation, impulsivity, aggression)
- confusion, memory problems
- mood swings (elation, mania)
- hallucinations (auditory, visual)
- feelings of dissociation (detachment, unreality, nightmares).

Are my symptoms those of withdrawal or a relapse?

Another problem is deciding whether symptoms that emerge on stopping medication are those of withdrawal or whether they are a relapse of depression. The following differences may help you and your doctor to decide which is the case.

1 Do your symptoms come on suddenly over days or within a week after stopping?

Withdrawal symptoms come on relatively suddenly within days to weeks of lowering or stopping an antidepressant. Symptoms of relapse of depression usually occur after one or more of stopping.

2 Are your symptoms physical

Physical symptoms such as feeling dizzy or light-headed, having flu-like aches, sweating, nausea, numbness, electric shocks and headaches are usually part of the withdrawal state. While some of these physical symptoms can occasionally occur in relapse of depression, they would have been part of the original symptoms you had, and you might recognize them as such.

3 How quickly do your symptoms improve when you stop medication?

Withdrawal symptoms peak within seven to ten days or so and are usually gone within three weeks; by contrast symptoms of a relapse of depression will persist and may get worse.

4 How quickly do your symptoms improve if you restart the medication?

Withdrawal symptoms immediately improve when you restart the drug. Symptoms of relapse may continue or get worse and take several weeks to improve when you recommence an antidepressant.

5 How do my doctor and I reduce the drug slowly enough?

The first step is to decide when to reduce the dose. This normally depends on whether you have been well for long enough and whether you are still vulnerable to relapse. Have you had an effective psychological therapy that can now protect you? The optimum rate of reduction of an antidepressant to a standard dose is related to the type of drug. In general, each reduction should take place over a month.

The rate at which you reduce the drug depends on the nature of the drug, the dose you are taking and the severity of any withdrawal symptoms you experience. For example, paroxetine (Seroxat or Paxil), which are prescribed at 20mg daily, might be reduced to 10mg for one month. Each reduction would then guide the speed at which the medication is further reduced. If withdrawal symptoms emerge, you may have to slow down. For example:

- if you experience mild or no symptoms then you need not change the rate of reduction (for example, paroxetine from 10mg to nothing)
- if you experience moderate withdrawal symptoms, the next reduction would be smaller (for example, paroxetine from 10mg to 5mg)
- if you have severe withdrawal symptoms your doctor may restore the original dose and then start smaller dose reductions (for example, paroxetine 20mg to 15mg for a month). If this resulted in no or mild symptoms, it could then be reduced to 12.5mg.

Most withdrawal symptoms can be minimized by reducing the drugs slowly, and this should be done under the guidance of your doctor. Some patients have been advised to take the drug on alternate days, but this does not make sense unless it is long acting like fluoxetine. It is nearly always better to reduce the dose of an antidepressant by a small amount on a daily basis. Further discussion on withdrawing from antidepressants can be found in the very helpful book *Coming off Antidepressants* (see Appendix for details).

Liquid preparations

To obtain smaller doses for a withdrawal program or to start at a lower dose, you can either cut the tablets in half or measure the liquid, which is usually easier. Alternatively, if you are simply unable to tolerate a tablet, you may find it easier to have your medication in the form of a liquid (an elixir). The drugs available as a liquid are listed in Table 15.1.

Use of medication in pregnancy and breastfeeding

Most of the SSRIs and clomipramine are generally considered to be safe for pregnant women. However, as no manufacturer wants to be sued, they all recommend 'caution' and say that their product should not be used in pregnancy or breastfeeding. No mother wants to cause harm to her baby, but in general there are no significant problems with these drugs. Fluoxetine, paroxetine, sertraline and clomipramine are the most studied in pregnancy or breastfeeding, so these are the most widely prescribed medication for pregnant women. Animal and human studies suggest a very low risk but are not fully conclusive. The risk of 'spontaneous abortion' may be very slightly higher than normal but the figures are difficult to interpret. Most doctors prefer to be cautious and treat health anxiety or depression with a psychological treatment where pregnancy is possible or planned. However, if you and your doctor believe that medications are necessary (and depression commonly gets worse during pregnancy), or if you find a psychological approach difficult, it is nearly always better for you to be functioning as a mother than suffering from depression, whatever the precise risks involved; but discuss this fully with your doctor since there may be new evidence that has appeared after the publication of this book.

What if a standard antidepressant fails?

There are other options if you do not get better with a SSRI or clomipramine. These options are best discussed with a psychiatrist. For example, there is some evidence for the benefit of combining different antidepressant drugs (for example, an SSRI such as citalopram with clomipramine). Sometimes a very high dose of a SSRI may be used. Alternatively, your doctor might recommend a different class of antidepressant, such as venlafaxine or mirtazapine.

Anti-psychotic drugs

Some doctors prescribe drugs for health anxiety that block dopamine receptors in a low dose either alone or as an additional treatment to a SSRI. These are also known as anti-psychotic drugs and include olanzapine (Zyprexa), ziprasidone (Geodon), risperidone (Risperidal), aripiprazole (Abilify), haloperidol (Haldol), quetiapine (Seroquel), sulpiride, trifluoperazine, pimozide and chlorpromazine. Some anti-psychotics (especially olanzapine and to a lesser extent risperidone) are more likely to cause weight gain and sedation.

Dopamine blocking drugs are normally used for treating psychosis and paranoia. There is no evidence for the benefit of dopamine blocking drugs either alone or in combination with another drug in the treatment of health anxiety.

Anti-psychotics might be prescribed in the short term if you are very agitated or for example have tics or have more complex problems with paranoia.

What are the side effects of dopamine blocking drugs?

In low doses, dopamine blocking drugs may help to reduce anxiety and do not usually cause problems. The main side effect may be tiredness. Some anti-dopamine drugs cause weight gain and loss of libido. When dopamine blockers are prescribed in higher doses, they can have side effects such as stiffness in the limbs or slurred speech that can be countered by medication such as procyclidine. A small minority of women may experience hormonal changes, such as stimulation of prolactin, which stops periods.

With a very high a dose or if you are especially sensitive, such drugs may cause abnormal movements such as a tremor and you may need other tablets to counteract them. They may also reduce libido. In general, an antipsychotic drug is not recommended in the long term for unipolar depression. In a higher dose it can emotionally numb you and prevent you from experiencing pleasure. If your main diagnosis is of unipolar depression and you are taking an antipsychotic drug, you may want to ask your doctor to review the drug.

If you are already taking such medication, then please don't stop or change the dose on your own. Always discuss your wishes with your doctor and plan things together. Do not be afraid to ask for a second opinion where necessary. Travelling to a specialized centre may be the most effective solution.

Tranquillizers

Tranquillizers are drugs that aim to reduce anxiety or are sedative. The most common are a group of drugs called benzodiazepines (diazepam or Valium, nitrazepam, lorazepam, clonazepam). Others are prescribed for sleep. There is no evidence for their benefit in treating health anxiety.

Tranquillizers used to be prescribed very commonly in the past but are less used now because of the risks of addiction. They are used for managing severe agitation in depression for the short term. The main side effects are slower reaction times, so they should not be used when operating machinery or driving. The main problem is dependence, so that a sudden withdrawal can lead to a short-term increase in anxiety, insomnia, irritability, headaches and many other possible symptoms. Withdrawing from such drugs therefore needs to be managed carefully.

Summary

In summary, medication can be an effective treatment in the short term for more severe health anxiety. It can be used alone but there is a high risk of relapse when you stop taking prescribed drugs if they are not combined with CBT.

It is important to discuss reducing or increasing your dosage with your doctor. Never stop taking medication without discussing it with your doctor first, and always ensure that you have another prescription ready before you run out of drugs.

Appendix 1

Finding professional help

When to consider professional help

A self-help book can be all that is required for some people to overcome health anxiety. After all, even with professional help, it is likely to be your own efforts between sessions that make the biggest difference. You might consider using this book with the aid of a professional; this is called 'guided self-help'. In this case the book can offer a shared way of understanding your problems, and the strategies to improve the way you feel.

Professional help, with an appropriately trained practitioner, is often the most effective approach. This involves working with a psychologist, psychiatrist, therapist, counsellor or nurse therapist. Cognitive behavior therapy (CBT) can help most people and rarely makes symptoms worse. We suggest that you seek professional help if your health anxiety is in the moderate to severe range, and especially if your attempts at self-help are not bearing fruit after a month or so. If you are feeling hopeless about the future and are having thoughts about ending your life, please seek professional assistance *immediately*.

Getting the right kind of help

If you are prescribed medication like Prozac, you can virtually guarantee that any pharmacy you go to will give you the right dosage and that the Prozac will be of the same quality. Unfortunately, this is not always true of getting the optimum psychological therapy. Of all the different forms of psychotherapy, only CBT has been shown to work for health anxiety and is likely to be the treatment of choice. In choosing a suitable therapist, the alarm bells to watch out for are therapists who:

- do not tell you what type of therapy you are receiving
- just keep asking 'How does that make you feel?'
- spend most of the time wanting you to discuss your childhood and the cause of your health anxiety
- do not share their understanding of what maintains your problem
- do not problem solve with you
- do not negotiate relevant homework between sessions
- do not monitor your progress in overcoming your symptoms.

If you are not sure, ask what type of therapy or counselling you are receiving. There is no evidence that general counselling, psychodynamic therapy, psychoanalytical therapy, hypnotherapy or transactional analysis is of any benefit in moderate to severe health anxiety. People may have found such approaches supportive or helpful for some issues but they are rarely helpful by themselves for overcoming health anxiety. Supportive psychological therapy may also help people to a degree in mild problems.

Similarly, beware of a doctor who offers only medication without also recommending a psychological treatment. You may find it difficult to get psychological therapies in state medicine because of the lack of funding: this is not the fault of the doctor, but a problem that requires political action and takes a long times to solve. In the meantime seek support, use the principles outlined in this book (or other CBT-based self-help material), and consider using medication if your symptoms are severe. In particular it is important to seek appropriate help – this may mean giving up the endless search for a physical cause of your problem.

Fears about seeking help from a therapist

You may have a number of worries about seeking help, such as:

What if it doesn't help?

It will be too embarrassing to tell them

They'll think I'm mad and want to keep me in hospital

What if they pass the information on to social services or my employer?

If you find it difficult to talk about some of your worries, it's usually helpful to say you are embarrassed or ashamed. Remember that worrying is normal and any health professional with the slightest experience in health anxiety will be sensitive to your difficulties. He or she will not consider you mad or want to keep you in hospital against your will. Individuals are assessed for detention only in *extreme* circumstances: if you are a danger to yourself or others (for example, if you are actively suicidal, neglecting yourself badly or are severely underweight). Such information is kept confidential and cannot be shared with other agencies or your employer without your permission. It does not go on any employment records or to social services. Only in *extreme* circumstances would a therapist ask someone to assess the impact of a person's health anxiety on his/her family and children (for example, neglect of your children's care because of your health anxiety).

A psychological treatment may not help initially because it can take a few weeks to take effect, but if nothing is risked nothing is gained and your problem is likely to persist for sometime. Furthermore, CBT or medications very rarely make your problem worse.

In teaching centres, you may be asked if a student or trainee may sit in. It is important to continue training others in psychological treatment but you are entitled to refuse without it affecting your treatment.

Remember, as with all other thoughts, try to treat your thoughts about seeking help as 'just thoughts' which are likely to be quite common under the circumstances. Rather than trying to ignore them, or debating them in your mind, take your thoughts with a pinch of salt and act consistently with pursuing your goal of overcoming your health anxiety.

Getting the most from a psychological therapy

You will get most from a psychological therapy if you:

- keep your appointments
- are honest and open with your therapist
- tell your therapist if you do feel very embarrassed or ashamed about your symptoms
- attempt the homework agreed between you and your therapist during therapy sessions.
- Having a good relationship with your therapist is important, but adherence to daily testing out of alternatives is the biggest predictor of success in therapy
- challenge your usual way of responding to your problem (for example, check, compare, brood, avoid) and act *as if* you have a thinking problem (even if you don't believe it)
- act against the way you feel and do it 'unconfidently' and 'uncomfortably' and are not sure it will work
- have clear goals that you want to achieve and you can agree on with your therapist
- regularly monitor your progress with the therapist by using the rating scales
- record the sessions so you can listen to them again
- give the therapist feedback.

You might find that you are not ready for CBT. If so, it may be better to return when you feel more committed to change and are able to do the homework regularly. Don't believe you are a 'hopeless case' – change is nearly always possible, then you can build on it. Don't be afraid to seek a second opinion or a referral to a specialist centre.

Types of professionals offering help

There are a range of mental health professionals who will offer help for health anxiety. Most mental health teams are multidisciplinary, which means that they include people from different professional backgrounds.

- Psychiatrists are medical doctors who specialize in mental disorders. They can prescribe medication for health anxiety and will probably be more knowledgeable about dosage and other issues required for health anxiety than your family doctor. Only a few psychiatrists are trained in CBT.
- Clinical psychologists have a basic training in psychology and have then trained in the clinical application of psychological assessment and therapies. They do not prescribe medication. Many will offer CBT but may not have had the specialist training and supervision required.
- Counselling psychologists have a basic training in psychology and are then trained in counselling and therapy. They do not prescribe medication. Some

may offer CBT but may not have had the specialist training required.

- Nurse therapists are originally trained in psychiatric nursing and in the UK most have specialized in CBT.
- Psychotherapists and counsellors come from a broad range of therapies. Most will listen to you and help you to work through issues in your life. They do not prescribe medication. They are not usually trained in CBT.
- All of the above may be suitably trained and supervised in CBT but will not have a lot of experience with health anxiety!

It is important to realize that, at the time of writing, there is nothing to stop anyone calling him or herself a counsellor or psychotherapist, whether he or she is properly trained or not. No therapist with a recognized professional qualification is going to mind you asking about his or her relevant training and qualifications. It is very important that you satisfy yourself about these things as well as the type of therapy used. What experience has he or she got of treating health anxiety (for example, the number of patients or clients he or she has treated)? What therapy do they use? If providing CBT, are they accredited or accreditable as having a minimum training in CBT? What are his or her expectations for change at the end of therapy and do these match your goals? Do you get on with the therapist? Of course you will want someone who is experienced in health anxiety, but if he or she is not, try to judge whether he or she is willing to learn more.

If you have problems with your therapist

If you want to complain about any professional, think clearly about the nature of the problem – for example, is it the type of treatment, the therapist, the location, or something else? Are there contributing factors – for example, the personality of your therapist or are you feeling more depressed? Can you sort it out with the therapist or another member of the team? Can you think of possible solutions to discuss with the professional? If the professional is refusing further therapy, listen to his or her reasoning and write down his or her explanation. If the reasons are financial (for example, it costs too much), don't give up since you may have to persist to get another opinion.

Finding professional help in the UK

If you would like professional treatment in the UK, your family doctor or general practitioner is the best place to start. He or she will usually be aware of what services are available locally. If you are worried about seeing your GP, take a relative or friend with you. If you find it difficult to talk to your GP, write a letter and give it to him or her. At your consultation, write down the key points that you want answered. You can always change your GP if you think you might be better understood or treated by another.

The information that you give your GP is confidential and cannot be shared without your permission. If your local mental health service is unable to assist, they may refer you to a national service. Unfortunately, getting referred to a specialist service can be a minefield in terms of funding and usually depends upon the support of your local mental health team. Communicate clearly that you need cognitive behavior therapy from a trained practitioner. For therapy services in the NHS, you can usually be referred only to a department and not to a particular individual. Despite this, you may find it helpful to do your own research and find out the names of recommended therapists from a support group or national charity.

In the UK, it is usually *quicker* to obtain help privately but it does not usually mean that the treatment will be any better. Good and bad treatment can occur both in the public and the private sector. It is best to do your homework and to ask for recommendations from your local support group or national charity, which may keep a directory of practitioners. In the UK, you can also try searching for a private accredited therapist on the website of the British Association of Behavioural and Cognitive Psychotherapists (http://www.cbtregisteruk.com) in the 'Find a Therapist' section. Not all cognitive behavioral therapists bother to become accredited and there are many from psychiatry, psychology or nursing backgrounds who are excellent cognitive behavioral therapists.

Finding professional help in the United States

In the United States, finding a cognitive behavior therapist may be difficult, depending on where you live. You could ask for a referral from your family doctor or recommendation from an academic psychiatry or psychology department.

The best recommendation may come from your local support group or charity. This is likely to be a member of the Association for Behavioral and Cognitive Therapies, which maintains a directory of therapists who can be contacted (http://www.abct.org). As in the UK, it is usually quicker to obtain help privately but it does not mean you will necessarily get any better treatment. Good and bad treatment can occur both in the public and the private sector.

Finding professional help in the rest of the world

The European Association of Cognitive Behaviour Therapists has a list of member associations on its website http://www.eabct.com. Details of the Australian Association of CBT can be found on its website at http://www.aacbt.org/.

Charities and support groups

In addition to professional help, national charities and local support groups can be invaluable. By joining and supporting them you can also help them. We do not yet know of any specific charities dedicated to health anxiety. In the UK, if you have health anxiety, then we recommend supporting OCD Action or one of the anxiety-based charities such as Anxiety UK. In the USA, if you have health anxiety, support the OCD Foundation.

By joining a charity, you will receive a newsletter and help put the issue on the national agenda. They also have information on local resources and support groups, which provide a forum for mutual acceptance, understanding and setting of goals. They will also be able to recommend local therapists or psychiatrists. People new to the area can talk to others who have learned successful ways for coping. Reading books about health anxiety and the Internet are useful ways of getting further information or support. The more you know about the problem and the more you can become your own therapist, the better equipped you will be overcome it. And when you recover your health anxiety, you can help raise funds for research into better treatments and campaign for better services and for training for more cognitive behavior therapists in public medicine. Unfortunately, many of the charities are too small and unable to focus enough energy on raising funds for research compared with the big charities in cancer or heart disease.

SPECIFIC PHOBIA OF VOMITING AND HEALTH ANXIETY SERVICE, BETHLEM ROYAL HOSPITAL

This unit provides a national specialist service for health anxiety and phobia of vomiting on the NHS. There are various referral routes. From a few areas we can receive a referral direct from a GP. However, for other areas the referral must come to us via your local Community Mental Health Team. A written referral should be sent to:

Dr David Veale
Anxiety Disorders Residential Unit
The Bethlem Royal Hospital
Monks Orchard Road
Beckenham
Kent
BR3 3BX
Tel: 020 3228 4146
Fax: 020 3228 4051

Appendix 2

International support groups and charities

We do not know of any specific support groups and charities for health anxiety. However, there are a number of groups for anxiety and obsessive compulsive disorder that often cover health anxiety.

AUSTRALIA

Anxiety Recovery Centre Victoria
Obsessive Compulsive and Anxiety Disorders Foundation of Victoria (Inc.)
42 High Street Road
Ashwood
Victoria 3147
Australia
OCD & Anxiety Helpline: 03 9886 9377
Office Line: 03 9886 9233
Website: www.arcvic.com.au
email: arcmail@arcvic.com.au

The Anxiety Recovery centre Victoria is an organization for people living with anxiety disorders.

CANADA

Obsessive Compulsive Information and Support Centre, Inc.
204–825 Sherbrook Street
Winnipeg, MB R3A 1M5
Canada
Tel: (204) 942-3331
Website: www.members.shaw.ca / occmanitoba /
email: occmanitoba@shaw.ca

This website provides assistance and education for people affected by OCD and related disorders such as health anxiety.

Ontario Obsessive Compulsive Disorder Network
PO Box 151
Markham
Ontario L3P 3J7
Tel: 416-410-4772
Website: www.ocdontario.org
email: info@ocdontario.org

OCD Ontario is a non-profit charity focused on providing help and information to children and adults with OCD and their families in Ontario.

NEW ZEALAND

OCD Support Group
Floor 2
Securities House
221 Gloucester Street
Christchurch 8011
New Zealand
Tel: +64 (3)366 0560
Website: http://OCD.org.nz/
email: info@OCD.org.nz

The website provides a place for people with OCD and their families to share common ground, information and support.

SOUTH AFRICA

OCD Association of South Africa
PO Box 87127
Houghton 2041
South Africa
Tel: 011 786 7030
Website: http://knowyourocd.co.za/
email: pserebro@iafrica.com

UNITED KINGDOM

OCD Action
Davina House
Suites 506-507
137–149 Goswell Road
London
EC1V 7ET
Office Phone: +44 (0)870 360 6232
Helpline: +44 (0)845 390 6232
Website: www.ocdaction.org.uk/
email: support@ocdaction.org.uk

OCD Action is a user led charity for individuals with OCD and related disorders like health anxiety and BDD.

OCD-UK
PO Box 8955
Nottingham NG10 9AU
United Kingdom
Office Phone: +44 (0)845 120 3778
Website: www.ocduk.org
email: admin@ocduk.org

OCD UK is a charity working with and for people with OCD.

Anxiety UK
Zion Community Resource Centre
339 Stretford Road
Hulme
Manchester M15 4ZY
United Kingdom
Tel: +44 (0)8444 775 774
General information: info@anxietyuk.org.uk
Website: www.anxietyuk.org.uk
email support service: support@anxietyuk.org.uk

Anxiety UK is a user-led organization, run by sufferers and ex-sufferers of anxiety disorders.

No Panic
93 Brands Farm Way
Telford
Shropshire TF3 2JQ
United Kingdom
Office Phone: +44 (0)1952 590005
Office Fax: +44 (0)1952 270962
Helpline:
(UK Free-Phone) +44 (0)808 808 0545
Non-UK +44 (0)1952 590545
Website: www.nopanic.org.uk
email: ceo@nopanic.org.uk

No Panic is a national charity that provides support for sufferers of anxiety disorders and tranquilliser withdrawal.

SANE
1st Floor
Cityside House
40 Adler Street
London E1 1EE
United Kingdom
Helpline: (0845) 678 000
Website: www.sane.org.uk
email: info@sane.org.uk

SANELINE is a national mental health helpline providing information and support with a database of local and national services.

THE UNITED STATES

Obsessive-Compulsive Foundation
PO Box 961029
Boston
Massachusetts 02196
Tel: (617) 9735801
Website: www.ocfoundation.org/
email: info@ocfoundation.org

The OC Foundation is a no-profit organization for people with OCD and spectrum disorders like health anxiety and BDD.

Appendix 3

Exercises

EXERCISE 4.5: THOUGHT-MONITORING CHART

In the left-hand column note your most common intrusive thoughts and images about your appearance, and then tick the relevant column (Mon–Sun) each time you have that thought, or add the total from your tally counter.

	Mon	Tues	Wed	Thurs	Fri	Sat	Sun
I have an intrusive thought that							
I have an intrusive thought that							
I have an intrusive thought that							

I have an intrusive thought that							
I have an intrusive thought image of							
I have an intrusive image of							

EXERCISE 6.4: MONITORING SELF-FOCUSED ATTENTION CHART

Date	Situation	% attention on self	% attention on task	% attention environment	Total (100%)	Distress (0–100%)

EXERCISE 6.6 RECORD OF ATTENTION TRAINING

Rating scale

−3: entirely focused on your own thoughts and feelings or the impression you have of yourself

0: attention divided equally between being self-focused and externally focused

+3: entirely externally focused on a task (e.g. listening to someone) or the environment (e.g. what you can see or hear)

Date	How self-focused I have been generally today (−3 to +3)	How long the training lasted	Number of sounds I used	Any other comments

EXERCISE 7.1: FREQUENCY OF CHECKING OR REASSURANCE

Date ____________

	Mon	Tues	Wed	Thurs	Fri	Sat	Sun

EXERCISE 7.2: HIERARCHY OF EXPOSURE TO FEARED TRIGGERS

Trigger (object, place, person, situation, thought, image)	Estimated distress (0–100)

EXERCISE 7.3: RECORD OF EXPERIMENTS FOR (DATE) ______

1 Task that I planned (e.g. when, where, how, and with whom. Include a description of how I will act without safety-seeking behaviors)	2 How distressing I am predicting task will be at the peak (0–100%)	3 How long I am predicting that the distress will take to halve (minutes or hours)	4 What I am predicting will happen or whether the result will best fit theory A or Theory B and how strongly I believe it (0–100%)

5 What I actually did during the task (including using any safety-seeking behaviors and degree of self-focused attention)	6 How distressing the task was at the peak (0–100%)	7 How long it actually took for the distress to halve (minutes or hours)	8 What actually happened? Does this differ from what I predicted in column 4? Do the results best fit my theory that I have a problem with my health or the alternative – that the problem is being excessively worried about my health?

EXERCISE 12.1: DAILY ACTIVITY SCHEDULE

Day/date:

Time	Activity	Time	Activity
7 am		4 pm	
8 am		5 pm	
9 am		6 pm	
10 am		7 pm	
11 am		8 pm	
12 pm		9 pm	
1 pm		10 pm	
2 pm		11 pm	
3 pm		12 am	

EXERCISE 12.2: PLANNED ACTIVITY SCHEDULE TABLE

Day/date:

Time	Activity	Actual activity	What was the effect of what I did on my emotions or the context in which I live?	Did it contribute towards my goals and valued directions in life? Rate it from 0–10 where 0 is not at all and 10 is extremely
7 am				
8 am				
9 am				
10 am				
11 am				
12 pm				
1 pm				
2 pm				

3 pm				
4 pm				
5 pm				
6 pm				
7 pm				
8 pm				
9 pm				
10 pm				
11 pm				
12–7 am				

EXERCISE 12.3: BROODING AND WORRYING SELF-MONITORING CHART

Week beginning ____________

Write in your most common brooding and worrying thoughts, and tick the relevant column each time you have that thought, or add the total from your tally counter.

	Mon	Tues	Wed	Thurs	Fri	Sat	Sun
I brood about:							
I brood about:							
I attack myself about:							
I attack myself about:							

Further reading

For health anxiety

Asmundson, Gordon and Steven Taylor, *It's Not All in Your Head: How Worrying about Your Health Could Be Making You Sick – and What You Can Do about It*, New York: Guilford Publications, 2005.

Barsky, Arthur and Emily Deans, *Stop Being Your Symptoms and Start Being Yourself: The 6-Week Mind-Body Program to Ease Your Chronic Symptoms*, New York: HarperCollins, 2006.

Cantor, Carla and Brian A. Fallo, *Phantom Illness: Recognizing, Understanding, and Overcoming Hypochondria*, Boston, Mass.: Houghton Mifflin Co., 1996.

Ehrlich, Richard, *The Healthy Hypochondriac: Recognizing, Understanding, and Living with Anxieties about Our Health*, New York: Holt, Rinehart and Winston, 1980.

Young, Charles and Brenda Hogan, *An Introduction to Coping with Health Anxiety*, London: Constable & Robinson, 2007.

http: // www.thehypochondriac.com

Emetophobia support and advice

There are a number of non-commercial websites and bulletin boards for people with emetophobia. Remember that some of the advice given for emetophobia by other sufferers may lead to keeping your fear going rather than overcoming your phobia and acting in your valued directions in your life. Support groups include:

Gut Reaction (http://www.gut-reaction.freeserve.co.uk)

International Emetophobia Society (http://www.emetophobia.org)

Emetophobics Proboard
http://emetophobics.proboards83.com/index.cgi

Fear of Vomiting
http://health.groups.yahoo.com/group/fov/

Fear of Vomiting www.fearofvomiting.co.uk

Emetophobia Listserv,
http://www.lsoft.com/scripts/wl.exe?SL2=16946&R=769&N=EMETOPHOBIA@LISTSERV.ICORS.ORG.

Books include *Living with Emetophobia: Coping with Extreme Fear of Vomiting* by Nicolette Heaton-Harris, London: Jessica Kingsley Publishers, 2007 (ISBN 9781843105367). This book was written by a person with emetophobia.

For general issues

Burns, David D., *Feeling Good: The New Mood Therapy,* Avon Books, 2000.

Fennel, Melanie, *Overcoming Low Self-Esteem,* London: Constable & Robinson, 1999.

Gilbert, Paul, *Overcoming Depression,* London: Constable & Robinson, 2009.

Gilbert, Paul, *The Compassionate Mind,* London: Constable, 2009.

Glenmullen, Joseph, *Coming off Antidepressants,* London: Robinson, 2006.

Hayes, S. C., K. D. Strosahl and K. G. Wilson, *Acceptance and Commitment Therapy: An Experiential Approach to Behavior Change,* New York: Guilford Press, 2003.

Meares, Kevin and Mark Freeston, *Overcoming Worry,* London: Robinson, 2008.

Silove, Derrick and Vijaya Manicavasagar, *Overcoming Panic & Agoraphobia,* London: Robinson, 1997.

Veale, David and Rob Willson, *Overcoming Obsessive Compulsive Disorder,* London: Robinson, 2005.

Veale, David and Rob Willson, *Manage your Mood,* Robinson, 2008.

Veale, David, Rob Willson and Alex Clarke, *Overcoming Body Image Problems including Body Dysmorphic Disorder,* London: Robinson, 2009.

Willson, Rob and Rhena Branch, *Cognitive Behavioural Therapy for Dummies,* Chichester: Wiley, 2005.

Zigmond, A. S. and R. P. Snaith, 'The hospital anxiety and depression scale', *Acta Psychiatrica Scandinavica,* 67/6, John Wiley & Sons: 1983: 361–70.

Index

Note: page numbers in italic refer to illustrations or examples. The letter 't' after a page number refers to tables. Where more than one page number is listed against a heading, page numbers in bold indicate significant treatment of a subject.